Quakers in Lewes

an informal history

Quakers in Lewes

an informal history

David Hitchin

2010

© David Hitchin
Second edition August 2010

ISBN 978-1-4461-4488-6

Acknowledgements

This book first appeared in 1984, the bicentenary year of Lewes Friends Meeting House, as a tribute to the men and women who established and maintained Quaker testimonies in the town. This edition adds new material which has since come to my notice, and now includes an index and bibliography for the main sources.

I am pleased to acknowledge the assistance of many people with this work. These include the staff of the East Sussex County Records Office, Sussex Archaeological Society, Lewes Public Library, and the librarians of Friends House in London, Malcolm Thomas and Edward Milligan. James Hodson allowed me to use an essay which he wrote as part of his undergraduate work. Without the genealogy produced by John Baily I could not have disentangled the complex relationships of the Rickman family. The University of Sussex allowed me time and computer facilities for the collation of material. Sharon Gretton and my wife, Diana, transcribed and indexed much larger quantities of information than is apparent from the size of this book. Many people have allowed me access to transcripts of diaries and other family papers.

Leslie Blomfield, Maurice Burge and C Walter Hodges provided illustrations. Other inset illustrations which are not credited individually are from histories of Lewes by Horsfield and Lower. Tom Reeves provided prints from negatives taken by Edward Reeves of Lewes.

I am grateful to the owners of copyright material for permission to reproduce it. The quotations in the account of the life of Thomas Hodgkin are taken from *Curator of the Dead: Thomas Hodgkin 1798-1866* by Michael Rose, published by Peter Owen, London, in 1981. Some of the accounts of the childhood of Maude Robinson are reproduced from the Sussex County Magazine by permission of T R Beckett Ltd.

Grants and donations to assist with the publication costs of the first edition were received from many sources, including the Barrow and Geraldine S Cadbury Trusts. I am grateful to them all, and hope that this revised publication will meet with their approval.

This book is dedicated to the members of the Religious Society of Friends at Lewes. It is on their faithfulness, over more than 350 years, that the existence of Lewes Meeting depends. The mode of business and worship are essentially unchanged since the beginning, but they still meet the needs of the present day, and the testimonies to peace, and to *that of God in every one* are now more relevant than ever before.

Contents

Acknowledgements	4
Preface	9
The Quaker Message comes to Lewes	11
Persecution	17
The First Meeting House	27
Legal Battles	35
Respectability	47
Quietism	57
The Twentieth Century	103
Bibliography	109
Index	110

Preface

Justices of the Peace and others in authority were much vexed by the extravagant and irritating proceedings of the new sect of Quakers. It is difficult to recognise in the conduct of some of these fanatics any resemblance to the dignified and orderly lives of their successors which secured for them the confidence of their fellow-citizens, and made them pre-eminently the bankers of the community. It bore some likeness to that of the more lawless advocates of "Women's Rights" in our own day.

C T Stanford wrote that in 1910 in his book *Sussex in the Great Civil War*. When one reads about early Quakers his harsh verdict may seem to be justified. What is there to explain the strange contrast between their contradictory reputations for bizarre excesses and for pedantic honesty? To answer this situation we have to look at the historical situation which gave birth to the Quaker movement, and then it will become clear that the apparently strange actions of the early Quakers were quite logical responses to the situations in which they found themselves.

Quakers have always documented their business meetings by minutes prepared during the meeting, read to the members and immediately signed. The Quaker concern for truth ensures the meticulous accuracy of these records, but the range of subjects minuted is often so narrow and the wording is so stylised that it is impossible to get any feeling for the personalities of the participants. Fortunately many Friends kept diaries, were prolific letter writers and kept detailed business records. Of course their concern with accuracy was not inconsistent with a biased viewpoint. Outsiders sometimes saw events differently, but as few of their records have survived this story is told almost entirely from the Quaker point of view.

Genealogists know how much care went into the compilation of Quaker records, and other historians have found much of value in them. During the periods of persecution the legal battles were recorded in a detail which will interest not only the legal historian, but anyone with a taste for court-room drama. For 200 years many Lewes tradesmen were Quakers, and a commercial history of Lewes which ignored them would be incomplete. The lists of fines which they incurred, goods which were taken from them and the possessions noted when they applied for assistance from Quaker funds, all provide valuable information about household goods and tradesmen's tools. The professional historian or the dedicated amateur who needs detailed information will go back to the original records.

Other readers should be aware that many of the passages quoted have been paraphrased. Some of the original documents were written in archaic English which does not make easy reading. This account retains the original words as far as possible, but spelling and phrasing have been modernised and much repetition has been removed. A few passages have been left unchanged to give a flavour of the originals. All quotations, whether literal or edited, are shown in a different typeface, e.g. *This is a quotation*.

Readers should also be aware that not all references are necessarily to the town of Lewes; the term *Lewes Meeting* refers not only to the Quakers who attend the Meeting House in Lewes, but also to the *Monthly Meeting*, the group of meetings over an area which at times included much of East Sussex and some of West Sussex. The records do not always clearly state which business related to which local meeting. When specific information has been lacking about the local meeting the gaps have been filled with information drawn from the other meetings, since the practice was quite uniform.

Writing a history like this is like trying to do a jigsaw puzzle which has many pieces missing. Some pieces have been joined together and seem to fit, but one or two may be in the wrong place. Where gaps exist we can guess what the pattern might be, and if the pieces are found our guesses might be proved right or wrong. Even if sufficient documents still exist for a thorough history of Lewes Quakers they might never be traced to the meeting house libraries, record offices and family archives where they are kept. There is still much work to be done, and I welcome the efforts of anyone who can correct or add to what I have written.

David Hitchin

The Quaker Message comes to Lewes

When Henry VIII came to the throne in 1509 England was a Catholic country, and Lewes was dominated by the church. A House of Grey Friars stood near Cliffe Bridge, and St Michael's College at South Malling was a great land-owner, but both were insignificant when compared with the Priory which possessed 19 parish churches, more than 20,000 acres and a monastic church longer than Chichester Cathedral.

When Henry died in 1547 the Grey Friars House was empty, the college had been closed, and the Priory had been destroyed. England became Protestant under the rule of the infant Edward VI, but returned to Catholicism when Mary succeeded him in 1553. During her reign 17 martyrs were burned at the east end of the market place in Lewes.

Lewes Priory ruins
Photograph by Diana Hitchin

In the next hundred years Acts of Parliament frequently required the clergy in the established church to change their beliefs and practices. Officially there were no martyrs in the reign of Queen Elizabeth; actually as many Roman Catholics died in her reign as there were Protestant martyrs under Queen Mary. Those executed were charged not with heresy, but with treason, since they acknowledged the Pope who was a foreign ruler.

As the Bible became more accessible and better known by all classes, controversy flourished within the Anglican Church between Episcopalians, Presbyterians and Independents. The Puritan movement grew, and eventually political and religious strife led to the Civil War. Men like the

Vicar of Bray could change their preaching and practice to reflect the changes in political climate, but men of integrity could not.

In 1662 the Act of Uniformity compelled many of the remaining ministers to leave their benefices. Under these conditions the seeds which had long been germinating sprang up. The Diggers, Levellers, Ranters, Etheringtonians, Grindletonians, Manifestarians, Fifth Monarchists and Muggletonians withered away, but the Baptists, Unitarians and Quakers took root.

The long period of religious strife explains more than the growing dissatisfaction which many people felt with the existing religious groups. It also explains why there were so many laws about religious practice. Each faction made its own laws to control its opponents, and although the earlier contradictory laws were forgotten they remained on the statute books. Eventually the enemies of the Quakers sought weapons to use against them and inventive lawyers resurrected old laws made for quite different purposes. The Friends were caught in the crossfire of almost forgotten battles.

Before we meet any Lewes Quakers we must make the acquaintance of George Fox, pre-eminent among the pioneers of the movement, since without him the behaviour of his followers would be incomprehensible. As a boy he was noted for his religious enthusiasm and his strict adherence to truth, but in his late teens he became severely depressed by the contrast between the faith and practice of the early church and that of the church around him. None of the religious men whom he consulted had anything to offer him and in despair he set out on a life of wandering, during which he seems to have memorised most of the Bible. Eventually several revelations, 'openings' as he called them, broke in on his mystic nature. He never questioned the authority of the Bible, but from that point on the ultimate source of authority was not in church or book, but in living experience.

Some of his insights now seem commonplace, but before his time they were almost unthinkable. He believed that *to be bred at Oxford or Cambridge was not sufficient to fit a man to be a minister of Christ. He forsook the priests and the dissenting preachers, and, when all my hope in them and in all men was gone, so that I had nothing outwardly to help me, nor could tell what to do, then, O then I heard a voice which said, "There is one, even Christ Jesus, that can speak to thy condition," and, when I heard it, my heart did leap for joy.*

He saw that *every man was enlightened by the Divine Light of Christ, and I saw it shine through all. In this I saw the infinite love of God. I saw also that there was an* ocean of darkness and death; but an infinite ocean of light and love which flowed over the ocean of darkness.

He mission was that of *walking cheerfully over the world, answering that of God in every one,* and this he did, preaching fearlessly in spite of repeated imprisonment and physical abuse to which he never responded in kind. Yet he was not a saint. He spoke with excessive zeal against anything or anyone who opposed his message, and he regarded any misfortune which happened to his opponents as the judgement of God.

Nevertheless he made thousands of converts, many of whom would give their lives for the truth, and none of whom responded with violence to the persecution which they suffered. In addition to his genius as preacher and mystic, he had a sound, practical approach to organisation which welded together inseparably the Quaker approach to worship and church business.

If Quakers had their origin in any pre-existing group, it was in the Seekers. They had little organisation, no clergy, no creeds, no sacraments and no ritual. They met on Sundays for divine worship, sitting in silence unless anyone felt moved to speak or pray, waiting for a revelation of the nature of the true church. George Fox took his message to these groups, and Quakerism sprang from his message and their practice. We know little of the Seekers who met in Lewes until, in 1655, their waiting came to an end.

An Account of the First comeing of the People of God (in scorne called Quakers) into this county of Sussex, and in what Places they first declared the Truth, and by whome they were first received, &c.

God, whose Mercyes are over all his Works, and hath Regard to the Cry of the Poore, and the sighing of the Needy in all Ages, and to the Breathing of his owne seed through all Generations, Did in this, our Day and Age, send forth his servants to Preach the Everlasting Gospell of Peace, and Bring the Glad Tidings of Salvation, and Redemption and Liberty to the Captive, and that the oppressed should be sett free, as people came to yield obedience to the heavenly Gift of God, the Light of Christ Jesus, as it was made manifest in them.

This Blessed Testimony and Joyful Tidings of Salvation was first preached in the north side of this county of Sussex, about the third month in the yeare 1655, at the Towne of Horsham, by John Slee, Thomas Lawson, Thomas Lawcock; and no man receiving them into his house, some of them Declared the Truth in the oppen market, in a powerfull maner Directing the people to yield obedience to the heavenly Gift of God, the Light of Christ Jesus, as it was made manifest in them; this was to the Great admiration of some. ['admiration' at that time meant amazement rather than approval] *Yet (as in all ages) the most part reviled, and some stoned them; others counted them mad men, yett all did not Daunt them, nor Stop their Testimony; but they bore all with such meekness and patience as was wonderfull to behould, and after haveing finished their Testimonys for that time, at that place, they Came the Same Day from thence to the house of Bryan Wilkason, who then Lived in a Park at Sedgwick Lodg in Nuthurst parish, about two milles from Horsham, who received them (he being, endeede, the first man that Gave Entrance as well to their persons as to their Testimony). This Bryan Wilkason came out of the North of England not long before, and the next day beeing the first day of the Weeke they had a meeting in his house, where thorow the power that attended their Testimony, the Witness of God in Some were Preached unto, and soe from that time Truth began to Spread it Self in the County of Sussex.*

The next meeting after that was at Ifeild the next first day following at the house of Richard Bonwick (a Weaver by Trade), who was the first that received them and their Testimony in that place, where was allso Convinced Richard Bax (since a Labourer in the Lord's Vinyard now Liveing at Capel, in Surrey), as allso Several others; and thus the Lord's work began to prosper.

Soone after that meeting held at Richard Bonwick's the same friends, viz., Thomas Lawson and Thomas Lawcock (and John Slee as is Supposed), Came to Twinham to Humphrey Killingbecks, and had there a meeting which was very Great and Servisable to the Convinceing of Severall and particularly John Grover, the Elder, William Ashfold, and Elizabeth Killingbeck, the Elder.

And about this time, viz., the 3ᵈ month in the aforesaid yeare, Came Thomas Robinson the elder, to the Towne of Lewis, and came to a Seeker's meeting held in Southover, near Lewis, at the house of John Russell, where he Declared the Truth to the Convincement of Ambrose Galloway, and Elizabeth, his Wife, and Stephen Eager, who were then members of the Said Meeting, and he was the means of Extinguishing of that meeting.

Soone after that came (that Memorable Man) Georg Fox, and with him in Company Alexander Parker, to the house of the aforesaid Bryan Wilkason's, where they met with Thomas Lawcock.

... After which they two, viz., Georg Fox and Alexander Parker, Came from that meeting at Stenning to Lewis, where they had again another meeting at the house of John Russell, in Southover, a Parish Joyning to Lewis, and they travelled from thence Eastward to Warbleton, and them parts. Quickly after which came Ambrose Rigg and

Joseph Fuce through this country and travelled much amongst us by visiting all the Meetings and served much to the establishing of them and continued their labours amongst us for several years.

The Croft, Southover High Street

For a while they may have been known to themselves as 'Children of the Light', or 'Friends of Truth', but the people of Lewes would have known them by the derisive name of 'Quaker', first given to George Fox. (The name 'Religious Society of Friends' cannot be traced before 1793.) Colin Brent has identified John Russell's house as The Croft in Southover High Street. The front of the house has since been extensively rebuilt, but it retains its original Horsham slab roof.

Persecution

The Society grew rapidly, but the activities of its members almost immediately attracted persecution. Charges were frequently brought against them for not attending church. There were laws against attending religious meetings other than the services of the established church. Informers who notified the authorities of breaches of this law were rewarded, and they were therefore tempted to offer false evidence, or at least to exaggerate what they had.

Friends refused to take oaths. Jesus said, But I say to you, *Sweare not at all ... But let your communication be Yea, Yea: Nay, Nay: For whatsoever is more than these, cometh of evil.* Friends also believed that using oaths on some occasions implied that a lower standard of truth was acceptable on others. This laid them open to prosecution for refusing oaths of allegiance. The law at that time did not give them the right to call council in their defence, to call witnesses or to cross-examine the prosecution witnesses. Such defences as they made in court had to rely on questions of law or technicalities in the wording of the charge since, without taking the oath, they were hardly able to testify to matters of fact in evidence.

When they refused to pay tithes their goods were distrained, often to a value much in excess of the amount due, as it was known that Friends were unlikely to seek redress for this through legal action. A final sanction was excommunication; a paradox as their crime was separating themselves from the established church, but the practical effect of this was to debar them completely from the protection of the law.

Friends testified against exaggerated and insincere displays of etiquette. A Justice of the Peace who had arrested George Fox visited him in prison. He doffed his hat and said, *"How do you do, Mr Fox? Your servant, Sir"* Fox replied, *Take heed of hypocrisy and a rotten heart, for when came I to be thy master and thee my servant? Do servants use to cast their masters into prison"* While others removed their hats in the presence of a superior, Friends removed their hats to no one, wearing them even in Meeting except when in prayer. They dropped the use of 'thou' and 'you' as indicators of rank, and insisted on 'thou' for one person, and 'you' for two or more.

Friends would not use the names of days of the week, as these were named after heathen gods, nor the names of the months, most of which were objectionable for similar reasons, apart from the last four which, after the reform of the calendar, were untrue – September, for example, is not the seventh month. Quaker dress was merely ordinary dress of the plainer kind, and had not yet become archaic, but the 'plain speech' and refusal of 'hat honour' made Friends immediately identifiable. Members of all of the dissenting denominations were subject to persecution, and it is likely that they suffered in larger numbers than Friends did, but only Quakers kept detailed accounts. Many of the following extracts are from these books of sufferings.

In 1658 they wrote: The inhabitants of this town have in these two yeares past dealt very cruelly to and wickedly with friends as they have come to and fro to their meetings, and in their meetings there hath been fire thrown in among Friends severall times to the danger of fireing the house, some friends receiving much wrong by the fire, and they have allso thrown in water, dirt and cowdung upon friends in their Meeting, and have broke the glass windows very much, and have beaten friends as they have passed to their meetings, and that in sight of an Officer of the Place who have been present, and beheld such things done as these, and have rather incouraged the wicked than endeavoured to keepe the Peace.

And at one meeting held in the old Castle Green at Lewis, the rude people, the sons of some of the Independents, with swords, guns, and pikes, running violently upon friends as they were kneeling downe in prayer, wickedly to disturb what they could, none of the officers of the towne seeming to take any notice at all of the abuse, or to appease the rude people.

Friends rejected the churches, on the grounds that their priests were 'hirelings' who had studied theology but had no experience of God in their lives. Quakers refused to speak of buildings as 'churches', following the New Testament in using the word 'church' only in the sense of the company of people who followed Christ. They referred to the buildings as 'steeplehouses'.

It was the custom in those days for divine service to be followed by public discussions, and Friends at first took advantage of these to debate their views with the preachers, although some impatiently interrupted before the sermon was over.

In this year [1659] Mary Akehurst, the wife of Ralph Akehurst, of the Cliff, neare Lewis, beeing moved to goe to St Michal's Steeplehouse (soe called), where an Independent priest [Walter Postlethwaite] was speaking, she for asking him a question, was by people haled out, and then sent for her aforesaid husband, who after she came home, did so hunch and pincht her, that she could not lift her arms to her head.

The same Ralph again on the seventeenth day of the third month of this present yeare, bound the hands and feet of his said wife and pinioned her, and then covered her very hot with bed-cloathes, and soe kept her for the space of foure or five houres; this it seems he did because she tooke occasion to reprove a hireling priest for belying her.

Againe, upon the twenty-fifth day of the eighth month, the aforesaid Ralph did sorely abuse his wife, on which the following lines were sent unto two Justices of the Peace (soe called), to complain of and to declare the same that she might not perish in private, but to lay it home to them, then in authority, viz.:

Whereas complaint hath beene made unto two of those who are in place to doe justice as, namely, Richard Boughton and Nathaniel Studly, of cruel persecution inflicted upon the body of a woman in the Clift, neare Lewis, by the hands of a wicked tirant, who is called her husband; his name is Ralph Akehurst, he hath chained his wife in a close back chamber in his house, between two high bed-steads, with a great chain much like a timber chain, containing thirty-five links, and a staple and lock, soe that this woman cannot move aboute the roome, or lye in the bed without this chaine, soe that with wait of itt it hath done much wrong to her legg, besides blows and bruses that he hath given her in executing his cruelty in putting on of this chaine, soe that thereby her body is much weakened at present, and murther may ensue if the Lord by his providence doth not some way for her deliverance; for this man hath promised that he will never unlock the chaine from off her, soe that in all likelyhood his heart is bent to destroy the body of this woman someway, for he hath attempted her life, as she hath said, by endeavouring to throatle her.

We set this forth to declare to the world, that if this woman shall putt off the body or sacrifice her life through his cruelty, that none shall hereafter upon just grounds say that she hath destroyed herself, or done any evil to her owne body, soe that if innocent blood be shead, we shall be cleare and the guilt shall remaine upon the heads which suffer such things to be done.

     Mary Akehurst
Subscribed by Mary Coulstock
     Ambrose Galloway
     Mary Dapson

This paper was not only sent to two justices, but a copy of it was placed on the church door in the Cliffe, and another on the market-house post in Lewis.

We do not know how this affair ended, but we do know that Ralph Akehurst died a few years later, while Mary's name appears again frequently in the records, as does that of her daughter, also Mary. Her sons, Ralph and Thomas imported cargoes of wine, flax, grain, pantiles, glasses, brandy and blacking through Newhaven.

After the Civil Wars there was a great shortage of small coins, and many traders provided tokens. Mary Akehurst's tokens were inscribed,:-
M*A 1637 – HER HALF PENNY – IN THE – CLIFFE NEARE LVEISTE, and others have survived from Ambrose Galloway's business.

In 1672 Mary was visited by William Penn who came *through much wet and dirt safe to Lewes, and are lodged at the widow Acres. This day being the first we had a good meeting. The Lord's Heavenly power was with us, and a good sense there was.*

This house in the Cliffe has been restored. Many houses in the 1660's would have looked like this

In 1660 William Holbem, Walter Scrase, Richard Scrase, John Wenham, Francis Randall, Thomas Brightridg, John Adams, Elner Robinson, Ann Cottingham, Elizabeth Hilton, Susanah Cooper, and Stephen Eager, for being at a peaceable meeting of Friends of Truth, worshipping the Lord in Spirit and in Truth, were committed to

prison by Sir John Stapley, and other justices (Soe called), and there remained until they were thence discharged the 9th day of the first month following 1660/1661.
[Traditionally the New Year began on Lady Day, March 25th, but January 1st gradually replaced it, and dates were written in both styles until the new calendar was recognised by statute law in 1752.]

James Mathew, John Scrase, Nicholas Yokehurst, Ambrose Galloway, Thomas Mills, William Yokehurst, William Gereing, Thomas Pettet, Henry Scrase, for being at a peaceable meeting of friends of Truth at Lewis, waiting upon the Lord in the way of his worship, were committed to prison by Richard Bridger and Nisell Rivers the 22nd day of the 11th month, 1660, and there remained until they were thence discharged the 8th day of the first month following, 1660/61.

In 1663 Ralph Richardson, an alehouse keeper, complained that Stephen Eager *"Did not go to the Steeple-house",* and he was thereupon called to appear at the sessions at Michaelmas *'soe called'*. So called, because Friends were already refusing to recognise the feasts of the church, just as they had abandoned the use of the 'heathen' names of the days and months. Eager, appearing before them, was asked if he went to Church and replied that he *"Did go to the True Church which was in God." After some words, they in their wrath to ensnare him asked if he would swear allegiance to the King.* He owned allegiance to the King, but would not swear, and was committed to prison where he remained for more than five and a half years.

It was Ambrose Galloway, a tailor, who kept the records of sufferings on which much of this chapter is based. He is not always easy to distinguish in the records from his son and grandson who bore the same name. The family had a shop just to the west of the bridge, and also owned property at the foot of School Hill. In 1664 Ambrose and his wife had been absent from church on four Sundays, as he was in prison and his wife had no one else to look after the children. A warrant was issued for four shillings, and on account of this William Bryant, a church warden of All Saints, took about forty ells of lockram. In 1670 George Tye, innkeeper of the White Lion, took two thin cheeses worth three shillings from Galloway as he had refused to contribute to the repair of the church. The sign of the White Lion is still visible on the town wall in Westgate Street, although the White Lion inn was demolished in 1937.

The White Lion

In 1670 William Snatt, the priest of All Saints, was owed two shillings and eight pence for two year's tithes. He sent his maid servant to Galloway's shop *for two fustian waistcoats worth eight shillings, but later refused to pay for them, and soe the unreasonable priest, for eight groats pretended due, had eight shillings.*

All Saints Church before it was rebuilt – the Meeting House just visible through the trees.

The name of William Snatt begins to appear frequently in the records. He became Rector of St Thomas's in the Cliffe in 1674, and then Rector of St Michael's and All Saints in 1675, until he left in 1681 to take a living at Cuckfield. He was determined to *root out the Quakers from Lewes*. Friends have left many accounts of attempts to prosecute them by due process of law, and also by sharp practice. *They reported that the priest, which is said to be a person of sober conversation, would often be drunk and stay up unseasonable hours in the night, and his conversation was with the wickedest men of the town and parish where he lived, and this priest whose name was William Snat did often joyne with wicked men to persecute friends, and he himself was an informer joyned with James Clark the Register, and he lived at Lewis till the yeare 1681, and was much hated by his own hearers for his wickedness, and did keep in his house a Crucifix and other Popish relics.*

Other sources show Snatt in a different light: Bishop Guy Carleton wrote that *Lewes is so factious a place that the good that Mr Snatt has done is remarkable*, and his ministry in Cuckfield seemed happier. He was clearly a man of principle and courage as he refused the Oath of Allegiance to William and Mary in 1689, and was deprived of his living as a result.

The list of imprisonments and fines is long. In 1664 several Friends were sentenced in a 'praemunire'. The Statute of Praemunire, of 1393, imposed severe penalties on those who appealed to the authority of a foreign ruler, especially that of the Pope, ignoring the English Monarch. In late times it was applied (with dubious legality) to various offences not connected with its original purpose. As Friends would not swear allegiance to the King it was sometimes perversely presumed that their allegiance was elsewhere.

A judge's outburst is recorded as follows: *At the Michaelmas Sessions (Soe called), at Lewis, in this yeare, 1664, Nicholas Beard, Richard Scrase, Walter Scrase, John Wenham, William Harrison, John Shutter, Thomas Avery, John Ellis, the elder, William Gereing, William Norton, Moses French, and John Martin, were sentenced in a praemunire, though very illegally, unjustly and ungodlily, by Philip Packer, judge of the court, who would not grant them a copy of their indictment, nor time to consider it, though they much desired it.*

But he, making haste to do them what mischief he could, passed a sudden and rash sentence, as it were, in a breath, in a broken confused manner, telling them that their goods and chattels were forfeited to the King for ever, and their lands and tenements during life, and their bodies to be imprisoned during the King's pleasure, or words to the purpose. He spoke in a disturbed spirit, that few knew whether it were in jest or in earnest, in wrath or in malice. He was so confounded in himself and his spirit or mind so distracted or unsettled that he passed sentence presently after upon a thief, that he should be stripped from the middle downwards, and whipped until the blood appear. But John Pelham, a Justice that stood by him, said from the middle upward, and then Judge Philip Packer said so too. He plainly appeared more fit to be taught than to be a teacher, much less a judge in such matters of high concernment wherein twelve men through his want of the true wisdom might have been ruined with their wives and children as to their outward estates and liberties, had not the Lord in His infinite wisdom provided better things for them, although ten of them remained prisoners on that account above five years or more.

In 1668 the Lewes Quaker meeting formally became part of the movement which was eventually to be named the 'Society of Friends.' The survival of the society is as much a consequence of the organisational genius of George Fox as of his spiritual insights. There are peculiar difficulties in maintaining a religious group with no stated creed, no paid clergy and following as far as possible the principle of equality among all members. Other sects destroyed themselves by internal dissension, or were brought into disrepute by individuals who claimed divine inspiration for their extreme teachings. Friends brought their revelations to their meetings for worship where their authenticity was tested against the experience of the group. Both in worship and business meetings the periods of silence had a moderating effect, often preventing direct conflict. No voting took place, or has taken place since, as the will of God is to be revealed by the Inner Light and not by force of numbers.

Each local meeting known as a Weekly Meeting was grouped with others to form a Monthly Meeting. The Weekly Meeting appointed representatives to the Monthly Meeting to ensure a presence, but in later years every Friend in good standing was entitled to attend. Every Weekly Meeting which was sufficiently large would have a session just before Monthly Meeting to consider any business which they should send forward, and so the term 'Preparative Meeting' became almost synonymous with 'Weekly Meeting'. A group of Monthly Meetings made a Quarterly Meeting, and at the top of the structure was Yearly Meeting. This organisation, almost unchanged since 1668, allows each individual Friend, as of right, to attend and speak at any level of the structure, from the bottom to the top. A central committee was founded so that speedy action could be taken to act for the society and relieve those who were suffering for Truth. 'The Meeting for Sufferings' has retained its name and function as an executive committee since that time.

The first Monthly Meeting for Lewes, Blatchington and Rottingdean was held on the 26th November 1668 at the house of John Wenham in Kingston. (John Wenham was a tailor who had lived in Southover before his death in Horsham Gaol in 1668. His will, proved in 1669, records that he had owned land in Kingston.) Although men and women worshipped together, from as early as 1677 there were separate meetings for business, partly on the grounds that men and women had different concerns, also to ensure that the women in their deliberations were not dominated by the men. Even so, there is little doubt that the women's meeting had less 'weight' in the affairs of the Society than that of the men.

The First Meeting House

At first, weekly meeting took place in private houses, but in 1675, at a Monthly Meeting in the house of Thomas Moseley in the Cliffe, it was ordered that *'the next meeting be held in Friends Meeting House in Lewes if the Lord permit.'* The building was completed in 1675, and in 1678 a lease was entered into by *Ambrose Galloway for all that messuage or tenement building, stable and garden with all the appertainances formerly known as Puddle Wharf.* The site, in Friars Walk, is about two hundred yards north of the present Meeting House. Some of the following extracts reveal that it was usually occupied by a Friend. This was probably a consequence of the Second Conventicle Act which gave the authorities the power demolish meeting houses. Turning a Meeting House into a dwelling house occupied by lease gave it some degree of immunity.

Quakers did not think of themselves as a sect. They believed that they were the true restoration of the early church and they expected to convert the whole world, which the power of the Spirit was bringing out of darkness into light. Therefore they did not recognise the existing churches, and, since marriage other than according to Anglican usage was not valid in statute law, they went to great trouble to establish their own careful practice.

The form of marriage was simple, but care was taken to ensure that the couple were clear of other engagements, and that adequate publicity was given at regular meetings for worship. Then, at a weekday meeting they would declare their vows to each other and sign a certificate to which all present added their names, a practice which continues unchanged to this day. In the early days at Lewes it appears that outsiders rarely attended Quaker marriages, so from those certificates we learn many of the names associated with the meeting; there were no formal lists of members at that time. Although the church denied the validity of such marriages, they were held to be good marriages in successive common law judgements and eventually the right of Friends to perform their own ceremonies was recognised in statute law.

Burial of the dead was another urgent necessity. William Holbem was buried in his own garden at Willingdon, but Lewes Friends arranged access to the Friend's burial ground at Rottingdean. In 1674 a deed provided for a 'burying ground' in Lewes, but the earliest recorded burial in Friars Walk was in 1697 when land had been obtained on a 1000 year lease from John Newnham of Barcombe.

The churchwarden's reports for Warbleton in 1676 mention both problems: *Elias Ellis, that hath been twice excommunicated, who refuses to pay his church tax, that hath in his grounds a burial place for the Quakers, hath taken a woman to his wife without any canonical marriage that we know of.* Elias Ellis later moved to the Cliffe.

This consolidation intensified, if anything, the efforts of the opposition. Certainly the existence of the Meeting House provided a focus. The townspeople of Lewes were unsure who owned, leased, or occupied the premises. When accused of holding illegal meetings, Friends often relied for their defence on such technicalities as errors in the name of the owner or lessee of the property concerned.

About the 7th month of 1675 was finished the building of the Meeting House of Friends, of Lewes, and on the 5th day of the 8th month following, William Snatt, priest, living in Lewes, accompanied with two other priests, and one Robert Smith, a tailor, came to a peaceable meeting of Friends held in their Meeting House at Lewis, William Snatt took the names of several that were there assembled, and went to Henry Shelley, called a Justice, and swore against several persons for being met together at the house of Thomas Moseley, which was utterly false (for it was not Thomas Moseley's house) and against a preacher, his name unknown, for which Thomas Moseley was fined twenty pounds, and the preacher twenty pounds, which fine for the preacher the Justice laid upon Nicholas Beard, of Rottingdean, ten pounds and for himself five shillings, and three pounds more upon Thomas Moseley, and upon Mary Akehurst, widow, seven pounds and five shillings, and upon Ambrose Galloway, for his wife being there, five shillings, and upon Elizabeth Shutter five shillings, and some other persons five shillings a piece.

Informers later gave information of a meeting in the house of Mary Galloway, but mark, this was the same house that Priest Snat swore but five days before to be the house of Thomas Moseley, and now he swears it to be the house of Mary Galloway, although there was no alteration concerning the said house.

On the 17th day of the same 8th month of this year, 1675, Friends being again met together, came James Clark, William Snatt and William Purser, with the constables, Ferdinando Bryant and John Delves, and a lieutenant and an ensign and two serjeants belonging to the militia, and also a great number of rude people of the baser sort, who, with great violence, dragged them out of the Meeting House, abusing many, drawing them in the streets, kicking, bruising, and beating many, and there was blood drawn from some, chiefly by the hands of James Clark whose beast-like behaviour caused many of the spectators to cry shame of him.

This being done, the informers went to Nisell Rivers, Justice, and gave information against several that were there assembled, and the justice imposed by his warrant these fines following ... for which James Clark took goods from Ambrose Galloway to the value of eighteen pounds and seven shillings, it being chiefly linen cloth, never measuring any. Ambrose Galloway was not at home when they rifled his shop, but he got leave of the man with whom the goods were lodged to measure the cloth that was taken, and so discovered its value, but he was not able to recover any of it. William Purser, the informer, should have put his own house in order: the churchwardens in 1675 and 1676 reported that he and *Anne Purser, wife of William Purser of All Saints in Lewes, had not been to church for eight months and three months respectively.*

On another occasion Ambrose Galloway and Mary Akehurst appealed to the Quarter Sessions. The informers were found to have perjured themselves and some Quakers had their goods restored. One informer fled Lewes, fearing prosecution for being forsworn *for had Friends intended anything of revenge they had advantage enough to have them brought to suffer the loss of their ears on the pillory. They rather chose quietly to take their own again, and to forgive the informers for that wicked act, thereby shewing them an example of innocency and self denial.*

In 1671 Ambrose Galloway was sued by William Kemp, of Malling, for a tithe on two acres of meadow land, a tenth of the estimated rent of three pounds a year, although Galloway considered the maximum rent to be no more than two pounds ten shillings, and said that the usual tithe was two shillings. While awaiting trial he was imprisoned, but the bailiff who briefly allowed him liberty to defend charges in the Bishop's court *was greatly blamed for suffering of him to come to make his defence.*

John Ellis, of the Cliffe, being fined four pounds, Clark took from him goods to the value of seven pounds and eight shillings. *Thomas Budd, a poor shepherd, being fined 25 shillings and not being at home,* Clark forced into his house and took away nine pieces of pewter, ten cheeses, a pottage pot, a skillet, a frying pan, and a bucket, with some other things, the bed hardly escaping, Clark wanting the tick to carry away the pillage in, but espying a sack took that and the bed escaped his hands.

From Thomas Robinson, a feltmaker, being fined twenty shillings, Clark took eight hats. Mary Akehurst was fined ten shillings. Clark took goods to the value of eighteen shillings. Mascall Picknoll, of Willingdon, being fined five shillings, Clark, without any officer with him (that he might the better cover his cruelty), took four rolls of linen cloth without measuring any, refusing to let them have it measured.

Upon the 24th day of the 8th month, 1675, some Friends being peaceably met together, there came James Clark, register, William Snatt, priest, and William Purser, informers, accompanied by the constables of Lewis and above twelve soldiers in arms belonging to the militia with their officer, without any regard to their Sabbath day, they drew Friends out of the Meeting House, abusing many with blows and cruel punches, and set a guard at the house door to keep them out. Then Clark demanded of Mary Galloway (who then dwelt in the Meeting House), a fine of five shillings for which he took seventeen new deal forms that cost near three pounds (which forms were not the goods of Mary Galloway, and loaded some of the soldiers with these forms, to carry them along the town whither he did direct. When many of the people and the constables were gone, Clark commanded one of the soldiers to break open the door of the house that he might use his will, there being none but two maids in the house. Thus did they continue for the space of four weeks with guards of soldiers to keep out Friends from meeting in their own house, in the streets in the winter season.

Also Clark did upon one of the first days demand another fine of five shillings of Mary Galloway, for which he took a new settle and five deal boards worth twenty shillings, which were not Mary Galloway's goods, but belonged to the Meeting House for the common service of Friends. This Clark being a very fat man would so labour at Meetings in pulling and thrusting of Friends and otherwise abusing of them, that he would often be in a great sweat, which in the winter time might have been prejudicial to his health, which he seemed in no way to fear, nor indeed the rage that he was in for the most part could let him think of it; but it pleased the Lord to continue him for further trial to Friends, as may appear in the following year.

Later the officers came into the shop of Ambrose Galloway (but then in the tenure and occupation of Ambrose Galloway, the son of Ambrose Galloway), who was not at the Meeting as charged, for which fine the officers broke open the counter and a press in the shop of Ambrose. They took away men's coats and breeches and children's coats and other goods to the value of twenty pounds five shillings and eleven pence, the said Ambrose being a salesman.

About the 5th day of the 12th month, 1677, died that notable persecutor of Friends, Edward Scripps, who made some profession of a cobbler's trade, and always lived meanly and poorly. As he had little power, (but what he had of his father, the Devil), he has not been taken much notice of in this book as many others have been, but for his exceeding villainies, which outpassed most in his lifetime, and his more exemplary death by the just judgement of God we shall here give some account of both, which take as follows:-

Edward Scripps several years before his death, daubed his own clothes with filth, and then came into a Meeting of Friends, thrusting and crowding himself among them on purpose to spoil their clothes, and threw dung in the face of the Friend that declared at that meeting. Not long after this action he was accused for [a crime obliterated from a Victorian transcript as unprintable], was sent to prison, and had a trial at

Grinstead Assizes. He was acquitted by the oath of a bailiff that swore prejudice in the witnesses, although the Judge declared he thought him guilty.'

And in the year 1675, Edward Scripps, being then a soldier in the trained bands, came to Friends Meeting House in Lewes, came to drag Friends out of the Meeting House, which he did with great violence, throwing some against the ground on purpose to hurt them. When they were out of the house and the door locked by them which dwelt in the house, he broke open the door with his musket. Friends continued the meeting in the street outside the door. Scripps brought wet straw and dung and set it on fire on the windy side of Friends as they stood and made an extreme smoke on purpose (saying he would make red herrings of them), to drive them from their meeting, and then put excrements in the keyhole of the door.

Soon after this he was cashiered by his captain for misdemeanours done to some of his fellows, and about the 5th day of the 12th month of this yeare, 1677, was hired by one Thurgood a butcher to fetch home a cow from Ditchling. There being a great snow as he came home, he was found about a mile from Lewes upon the downs, thus ended he his miserable life and no repentance ever known by any.

On the 5th day of the first month of 1678, Thomas Harrison, grocer, of Lewes and constable of that town, accompanied with James Clark and Walter Joans, the old informers and persecutors, and Richard Page, mass-house warden, came to a meeting of friends held in their usual Meeting House in Lewes, to wait upon the Lord, and Nicholas Beard being then in prayer to the Lord, Clark, as his old custom was, laid violent hands upon him and dragged him about the house upon his knees in a most inhuman manner.'

On the 24th day of the 6th month of 1679, Friends being met together at their Meeting House according to their usual manner, there came into the meeting Edmund Middleton and John Tuck, constables of Lewes, with Richard Page and John Halcomb, steeple-house wardens, with many others of the baser sort of people, and with them came also Samuel Astie, a proctor to the Bishop's Court, and Thomas Barratt, who was then servant to James Clark, and these two took in writing the names of several Friends. With the help of the officers and people, in a most violent manner they pulled down John Songhurst, who was speaking to the people of the things of God, and then fell upon the rest of Friends, pulling, throwing on the ground, and haleing out of doors most of the meeting, not unlike to the worrying of harmless sheep by a senseless dog, set on by his master, as they were by theirs.

Then some of the people found Henry Gates declaring in the Meeting more of the things of God. They pulled him down, and abused him with many others, and then retreated. Friends held on their meeting, but many of the people coming the third time, and finding Nicholas Beard at prayer to the Lord for themselves and enemies, Samuel

Astie struck him twice on the mouth and face, and thrust a stick or cane on his stomach to stop his breath, or do him some mischief, and then Middleton, the constable, and others laid violent hands on him, and pulled and thrust him head down foremost that he fell on his head, which, had not the goodness of God prevented, might have done him much harm (he being aged and heavy), some of them saying that if they would not go away the blood should run.

Now the chief of those who were helpers are as follows:- John Postlethwaite, John Vandike, the younger, and Richard West and William West, and Thomas Wood, a barber chirurgeon. These four last were all of the Cliffe, near Lewes, and were not officers, but all had their several places in the Devils employ of pulling and haling Friends, in which they did their utmost, and so are as worthy as most in their rank of persecutors, among whom if they should not be afforded a place they would be wronged.

The first recorded reference to the Friend's peace testimony dates from 1680, when Thomas Robinson was taken to court for not paying *two pence, the tax for maintenance of drums and colours which for conscience sake he refused to pay them. They therefore distrained from him three pounds of shoemaker's hemp, to the value of three shillings and six pence. John Ellis, being taxed three pence, they distrained from him a pair of stockings to the value of about fourteen pence. Thomas Moseley was also taxed three pence, which for conscience sake he refused to pay at their demand, for which they distrained from him a piece of filleting to the value of two shillings.*

The peace testimony did not exist when the Society of Friends began; there is a lively debate among historians about the number of early Friends who had served in the army, and there were serious attempts to persuade George Fox to accept a commission. It is little known, although perhaps not surprising, that some early Friends did not accept this part of what became the corporate view. Newhaven port records reveal that the Galloway family were involved with the export of Wealden cannon, and did business with the Wealden iron masters. Monthly Meeting records report that Friends were sent to *deal with Ambrose Galloway,* although the nature of the dealing and the outcome are not reported. In 1677 the meeting considered Walter Norman, who was employed boring guns at Maresfield, but they left the matter to his conscience. Many years later the Galloways fired cannon from a raft moored in the Ouse to support John Fuller when he sought election as a Tory Member of Parliament.

Friends never responded to physical violence to the aggression directed against them, but their behaviour was not above reproach. In 1681 Monthly Meeting decided that *touching the difference between Mary Akehurst and Ambrose Galloway the Younger concerning her children scoffing at people on the fast days as they* went to the steeplehouse, it is the sense of the Meeting that Mary has wronged Ambrose in saying he was a liar, when upon enquiry for the author it was found otherwise.

There is a note of bitterness in the following accounts of the deaths of their persecutors.

And here it may be noted as an example to wicked men, that about the year 1681, John Coppard, bailiff, who arrested Thomas Moseley, was one day in the summer time digging chalk out of the pit in the Cliffe, and it is supposed that he had been drinking. He unadvisedly struck on the chalk which hung over his head, and it fell down on him and beat out his brains. He was not seen to move after it.

Just at the beginning of 1682 James Clark went to Chichester and at his return home soon fell sick, whether occasioned by that journey or by his debauchery (to which he was much addicted), and not so much for love of company as to wine and brandy, which he would drink and guzzle down in a very inordinate manner in his own house without any company. However it pleased God to cut him off from being a further scourge to his people in this persecution, for in four or five days sickness he died, being altogether senseless for two or three days, so that he was not capable to make any will, or disposal of what he had, and in the time of sickness was visited by such as were of his company when in health. So ended his miserable life without any seeming remorse of conscience for all his wicked deeds done in the County of Sussex, as well as to most sorts of other people, as to Friends. Leading a very sottish life and being a fat man he was often like to be choked with a rising in his throat which he usually passed over by drinking a glass of sack, but now a glass of sack would not do it. It proved mortal to him so he died on the twentieth day of the eighth month of this year and the other two informers, not taking notice of the judgement of God in cutting off that wicked persecutor, still go on with their work of informing just begun before his death.

Legal Battles

On the 6th day of the 10th month, 1682, Samuel Astie by the order of Henry Shelley, justice, delivered the following papers:-

Sussex Sessions.
    To *Ambrose Galloway*, the elder of *Lewes*, tailor, *Thomas Moseley*, of *St Thomas in the Cliffe*, woollen draper, *Elizabeth*, wife of *Thomas Robinson*, felt maker, and *Thomas Akehurst*, of the same parish, mercer, and *Henry Gates*, of *Cuckfield*, yeoman.
    Whereas, *John Eresby*, and *Samuel Astie*, notary public, both of *Lewes*, have this present day taken their corporal oaths before me, *Henry Shelley*, one of Her Majesty's Justices of the Peace for the County of *Sussex*, that upon Tuesday, the 10th Day of October last past, an unlawful conventicle or meeting was held in a house called *Puddle Wharf*, in the Parish of *All Saints* in *Lewes* under colour and pretence of exercise of religion, in other manner than according to the liturgy and practice of the Church of England, and that *Henry Agates*, then and there did take upon him to preach or teach in the conventicle, assembly or meeting, contrary to the laws and statutes in that case made and provided, and *Ambrose Galloway*, the elder, *Thomas Moseley*, *Elizabeth Robinson*, and *Thomas Akehurst*, were at that time hearers of, and present at, the pretended exercise of religion.
    These are therefore to give notice and warning to you and every one of you that I do intend to hear the said cause at my house on Friday next ensuing the date hereof, between the hours of three and four of the clock in the afternoon, where you and every one of you may be present, if you will, and show cause, if you can, why you, and every one of you, should not be convicted of the offences and fines or sums of money forfeited thereby, be levied upon you for the same, according to law. Given under my hand and seal of 6th day of November, 1682.
HENRY SHELLEY

    Friends replied, denying that they had been at any conventicle or unlawful meeting on that day, and saw nothing unlawful done in that house. They asked the informers to state exactly what they alleged had been said or done against the liturgy or practice of the Church of England. They also pointed out that the law did not forbid all meetings, and that the meeting which they had attended would only have been illegal if they had done some illegal act. To meet to seek God's guidance was not illegal, and the liturgy itself said *it is both meet and right and our bounden duty at all times and in all places to give thanks and praise to Almighty God.* They argued that speaking and preaching are not the same thing, and that their speaking should not be counted as preaching unless the informers could prove that scripture had been expounded. Finally they denied that they knew any Henry Agates who had preached. (They all knew Henry Agates, otherwise known as Henry Gates, but he had not preached that day).

When they appeared before Mr Justice Shelley they demanded of the two informers what words they heard preached at the said pretended meeting, but the informers seemed loathe to say. At last, with much bogling, the priest said he heard Henry Gates preach that the soul of man was of great concern, and then Ambrose Galloway answered that 'they might convict them for that, but the priest had little to say for himself, nor could not deny the truth of them words.' Yet, notwithstanding all that they could say in their own defence, together with the small account that they informers could give, the Justice issued his warrant, imposing fines, upon Henry Gates the sum of twenty pounds for preaching, and upon Ambrose Galloway, Elizabeth Robinson, Thomas Akehurst, and Thomas Moseley, upon each of them the sum of five shillings for being present.

And on the same day for the fine of five shillings imposed on Thomas Akehurst, they took a small cask of soap, to the value of seven shillings. Richard Knight intended to have gone in as he had done at Thomas Moseley's shop, but by a strange providence was hindered before the soap was distrained, as just at his stepping into the shop his foot slipped and he broke and put out of joint his leg, and was fain to be carried home by men. Yet, notwithstanding, the rest failed not to carry on the wicked work.

Friends refused to pay tithes on a principle which now is easy to understand, but others were simply tax evaders. Church officials may have seen no difference between Friends and the splendidly contumacious John Farley (not a Quaker) who lived in South Street in the Cliffe *and had there bought a small cottage which for the meanness thereof had never been chargeable with any tax. Now John Farley had pulled down that shed and on the same ground built a good tenantable house worth four pounds a year, for which the priest demanded tithes. Being denied by John Farley, he proceeded against him for non payment in the Bishop's Court of Excommunication.*

John Farley took no notice thereof, but came again to church (called), as he was wont to do, where John Eresby was preaching. The sight of an excommunicate person interrupted him, so he commanded John Farley to be hauled out of the steeplehouse, which was done once or twice. The old man came in again, alleging that he had gone to church for forty or fifty years or more and would not now be hindered, which caused a further disturbance. One Thomas Wood, the overseer of the poor, beat John Farley in the steeplehouse, and beat out one or two of his teeth, and the priest to do the business more effectually came out of the pulpit to help get him out, which with the noise of the men scuffling together, and the fear and hurry the people were in, caused many of them to depart, and soon after the priest followed all in a confusion, (or else he must have preached to the walls). This course John Farley held on for several days.

And other days when the priest went to the steeplehouse he has been fain to go to some other steeplehouse hearing that John Farley was got in there. Sometimes by fair means and flattery he desired John Farley not to disturb him, and promised him an absolution for nothing, which when John Farley went to demand it, would not be granted (except he would pay the charge of the court, which he refused to do). The priest having a desire to be quiet on that day called Christ mass day, to perform their wonted service in the steeplehouse of the Cliffe, sent the following warrant to John Heaver, then steeplehouse Warden.

To the churchwardens of the Cliffe
    Since there is no other course to be taken with Goodman Farley, but down right force, and since your office does oblige you to see that no excommunicate person come into the church, these are to command and charge you that you take care Farley make no disturbance; which to prevent, you are both to stand at the entrance, and not suffer him to approach.
John Eresby
December 25th, 1682

The priest made offers for a composition with John Farley, offering to abate him a great part of the money first demanded, but no end could be put to it till the next sessions following, when some justices (on petition of John Farley), took up the business, so that he was readmitted into the church. If the priest's envy and rash proceedings had not turned him out that labour for an indulgence might have been saved.

On the 5th day of the 10th month, 1682, Friends being met together to wait upon the Lord in their usual Meeting House in Lewes, the informers, John Eresby, the priest, and Samuel Astie, the proctor, came in amongst them, and took the names of Thomas Robinson, Ralph Akehurst, Thomas Akehurst (who was not at the meeting), Benjamin Moseley, Henry Agates alias Gates, and went to Henry Shelley and informed him thereof, whereupon Justice Shelley issued a summons:

Sussex Sessions
To Jane Kidder, of Lewes, Spinster.

Whereas, John Eresby, Clerk, and Samuel Astie, of Lewes, Sussex, have formerly taken their corporal oaths before Henry Shelley, Esquire, on of his Majesty's Justices of the Peace for the county of Sussex, that upon Tuesday, the 10th day of October last past, an unlawful conventicle or meeting was held in a house called Puddle Wharf, commonly reputed the house of you Jane Kidder, in the parish of All Saints. These are therefore to give you notice and warning to you that you may have a personal hearing of the cause before Henry Shelley, Esquire, at his house in Lewes, between the hours of three and four of the clock in the afternoon of this present 5th day of December, 1682, and where you may shew cause, if you can, why you should not be convicted of the crime aforesaid, and the sum, fine, or sums of money forfeited thereby be levied upon you for the same, according to law.

By the order of the said Mr. Shelley,
Sam Astie
December 5th, 1682

    This summons to Jane Kidder was for that same day, but the rest of Friends were not to appear till some days after. The informers being impatient of their prey went before the day of appearance came to Richard Bridger (called) a Justice, and there they gave him information against the same they had done before to Justice Shelley, and about eighteen more unknown, which now they swore also to have been there. Richard Bridger imposed fines as follows:-
    On Henry Gates, of Cuckfield, for his second offence (called) of preaching, forty pounds. On Thomas Akehurst (although at neither of the meetings) for his second offence ten shillings. And twenty pounds fine for the house, with five shillings a piece as hearers, was laid upon Thomas Robinson, Benjamin Moseley, and Ralph Akehurst, but by reason the warrant came not to the hand of Friends, we are not certain as to each one the particular sum to be levied.
    But here it may be observed that the first warrant granted by Henry Shelley was not as yet levied (which imposed on Henry Gates the sum of twenty pounds for the meeting held the 10th day of the 8th month 1682). These informers wanted to have both the warrants to execute together. When they had this last warrant for forty pounds the informer, Samuel Astie, and Caleb Fuller, of Fletching, assisted by the constable of Cuckfield, went to the house of Henry Gates, and in a most rude and threatening manner demanded for the two warrants three score pounds, which not being paid they seized fatting beasts, which were a few days before bought by butchers, and other goods. Not being satisfied with what they had, they returned for another warrant:

Sussex Sessions
— *To the Constables, Headboroughs, Church-wardens, and Overseers of the poor for the Parish of St Thomas in the Cliffe.*

Whereas, Ralph Akehurst and Thomas Akehurst, both of the said Parish of St Thomas in the Cliffe, mercers, and Thomas Robinson, of the same parish, feltmaker, together with several other persons, were met together in an unlawful assembly or conventicle, contrary to the form of the Statute in that case made and provided, in a house called Puddle Wharf, within the Parish of All Saints, in Lewes and in the occupation of Jane Kidder, spinster, on Tuesday the 5th of December, and have been duly convicted thereof before Richard Bridger, esquire, one of her Majesty's Justices of the Peace, by the oaths of John Ereseby, clerk, and Samuel Astie, notary public, both of All Saints, and because the sum of twenty pounds are forfeited by law, become due from Jane Kidder, for wittingly and willingly suffering the unlawful conventicle to be held but Jane Kidder, by reason of poverty and inability, cannot satisfy the said sum, I have therefore imposed the sum of nine pounds and fifteen shillings of good and lawful money of England upon Thomas Robinson, being part of the sum of twenty pounds forfeited from Jane Kidder.

I have likewise imposed the sum of five shillings apiece upon Ralph Akehurst and Thomas Robinson, for being present at the unlawful conventicle, assembly, or meeting, and because Thomas Akehurst was formerly convicted, I have therefore imposed the sum of ten shillings upon Thomas Akehurst, for his second offence.

These are therefore in the King's name, to will, require, and command you and every of you respectively that upon sight hereof that you levy by distress and sale of the goods and chattels of Ralph Akehurst, Thomas Akehurst, and respectively imposed as aforesaid, and upon receipt thereof you are hereby required and commanded to pay the same in unto me that I may dispose thereof according to the directions of Act of Parliament in that behalf; and hereof fail not at your peril.
John Stapley

Another warrant was issued to the constables to levy the fine of ten pounds imposed on Benjamin Moseley, and a smaller fine on Jane Kidder. They went to Moseley's shop but looking more closely at the warrant they realised that a warrant already existed for the offence named so they left the shop without taking anything. The officers of the Cliffe were less particular:

For, about the 6th day of the 11th month of 1682/3, Richard Stonehors, Constable, and John Olive, Headborough, with Thomas Wood, Overseer of the poor, and John Heaver, steeplehouse warden, came to Thomas Robinson's shop, and by colour of the said warrant seized and carried away eighty hats, to the value of thirty pounds, nineteen shillings, which were carried to the Red Lion to the house of Richard Knight, with the rest of Friends' goods.

Thomas Robinson, aggrieved by these illegal proceedings, since Justice Shelley had issued a third warrant for the same offence, and as the informers had perjured themselves, entered an appeal on the 9th day of the 11th month, as follows:

Whereas, Richard Bridger, Esq., one of his Majesty's Justices of the Peace has upon the oath of John Eresby, clerk, and Samuel Astie, notary public, convicted Thomas Robinson, of the parish of the Cliffe, of being present at a conventicle or meeting at a house in All Saints in Lewes, in the occupation of Jane Kidder, spinster, on the 5th day of December last, under colour of exercise of religion in other manner than according to the liturgy of the Church of England, and whereas Sir John Stapley, Knight and Baronet, one other of his Majesty's Justices of the Peace, has upon Richard Bridger's conviction by his warrant under his hand and seal, bearing date the first day of January instant, imposed upon me five shillings, for being present at the conventicle or meeting; and in respect of the poverty of Jane Kidder, has likewise imposed upon me the sum of nine pounds and fifteen shillings more, for her suffering a conventicle or meeting to be in her house, which sums of money were, by virtue of Sir John Stapley's warrant levied on my goods and chattels on Wednesday, the 3rd day of January instant; now I do hereby appeal from conviction of Richard Bridger, to the judgement of the Justices of the Peace, in their next Quarter Sessions, to be held for the East part of the County of Sussex. In witness whereof, I have hereunto set my hand, the 9th day of January, 1682.

On the 11th day of the 11th month of 1682 began the Quarter Sessions, held at Lewes, where the matters transacted in relation to Friends were as follows:

Some time past, before the sessions, John Eresby (the informing priest of Lewes) came into the shop of Thomas Robinson, in the Cliffe, and cheapened a fine caster hat, to the value of fourteen shillings, and after some slight discourse, carried it away by force, telling him that he took it for Parson Snat. Thomas called after him, 'Stop, thief.' Notwithstanding, there was no getting of it again. Whereupon, Thomas Robinson, for recovery of his right (and not for revenge) indicted him the first day of the sessions, for a trespass. He was found guilty, ordered to pay the charge of the Court, and Thomas Robinson for his hat, and so was discharged.

And the next day, being the second day of the sessions, John Eresby, priest, and Samuel Astie, proctor, and both informers, were jointly indicted by Friends as they had wickedly and maliciously sworn wrongfully against Thomas Akehurst thereby making him guilty of being present at two meeting, (when there was sufficient witness to prove that he was at home all the time of the meeting), a false oath, so often repeated before several magistrates. This bill of indictment for perjury preferred against them by Friends, was found to be a true bill by the jury.

Another jury tried the appeal by Henry Gates. The statute applied only to meetings at which five or more people were present. Without Thomas Akehurst there would have been only four, and only an hour before the witnesses to his presence at the meeting had been convicted of perjury. Nevertheless the jury found that he was present – on the evidence of the same witnesses.

But the court ordered the Constable to return the fourscore hats which were taken from Thomas Robinson. On the same 12th day of the 11th month, 1682, the priest Eresby, and Samuel Astie, informers, indicted most people about the town of Lewes that did not go to the steeplehouse, to the number of near one hundred. Friends were indicted separately, and the jury rejected the bills against other dissenters as they were not certain that they would not go to church, but, as for the Quakers, they knew that they would not. So they found the bills against the several persons following, viz., Henry Gates, Ambrose Galloway, senior, Thomas Moseley, Ralph Akehurst, Benjamin Moseley, Nicholas Beard, senior, John Ellis, of Warbleton, Elizabeth Robinson, for being absent from church (called) for the space of one month, and for being present, some at the meeting on the 10th of the 8th month, 1682, contrary to the Statute made in the 35th year of the late Queen Elizabeth. The bill found against them was a trap laid by the wicked informers to take away their lives, but the Lord delivered them.

The persons hereunder named were also indicted, and the Bill found against them:

Thomas Robinson
Ambrose Galloway, junior
Ruth Galloway
Elizabeth Galloway   for absenting themselves
Thomas Beard   from Church (called) for
Mary Akehurst   the space of nine months.
Thomas Akehurst
Alexander Akehurst
Jane Kidder

Jane Eager was indicted for three months.

At this point it may be interesting to see just how the *Statute made in the 35th year of the late Queen Elizabeth* related to Friends. There were, in fact, two statutes, parts of which read as follows:-

For the preventing and avoiding of such great inconveniences and perils as might happen and grow by the wicked and dangerous practices of seditious sectaries and disloyal persons; be it enacted that if any person above the age of sixteen years, which shall obstinately refuse to repair to some church, chapel, or usual place of common prayer, to hear divine service established by her Majesty's laws ... That then every such person, being thereof lawfully convicted, shall be committed to prison, there to remain without bail or mainprize. Provided also, That every person that shall abjure by force of this Act, or refuse to abjure being thereunto required as aforesaid, shall forfeit to her Majesty all his goods and chattels to ever; and shall further lose all his lands.

For the better discovering and avoiding of such traitorous and most dangerous conspiracies and attempts, as are daily devised and practised against our most gracious Sovereign Lady the Queen's Majesty and the happy state of this Commonweal by such sundry wicked and seditious persons, who terming themselves Catholics and being indeed spies and intelligencers not only for her Majesty's foreign enemies but also for rebellious and traitorous subjects born within her Highness' dominions, and hiding their most detestable and devilish purposes under a false pretext of religion and conscience do secretly wander and shift from place to place within this realm, to corrupt and seduce her Majesty's subjects, and to stir them to sedition and rebellion ...

And be it further enacted, That if any person which shall be suspected to be a jesuit, seminary or massing priest, being examined, shall refuse to answer directly and truly whether he be a Jesuit or [&c] as is aforesaid, every such person so refusing to answer shall be committed to prison until he shall make true and direct answer to the said questions whereupon he shall be so examined.

The Acts were directed against Catholics, but lawyers used them as precedents for the prosecution of Quakers. Perhaps the prosecutors were attracted by the draconian penalties permitted by the Act. It may seem incredible now that the authorities should confuse the Quakers with the 'Jesuits and massing priests.' The authorities maintained that the Quakers could easily identify themselves by 'answering directly and truly', but this had to be done on oath and the Quakers would not swear.

When the Sessions began in Lewes on the 19th day of the second month of 1683 the parties indicted at the previous Sessions were called, most of them for nine month's absence from church. Friends claimed that the court was not competent to deal with the offence. This plea was entered in Latin, engrossed on parchment and signed by Councillor Darnell. Councillor Henry Bish tried to enter a demurrer [a statement agreeing to the facts, but denying legal liability] *to the plea, but it was not accepted, and the indictment was withdrawn.*

In consequence John Eresby and Samuel Astie brought in a certiorari [an appeal to a higher court against the procedure in a lower one] *to remove the counter-claim which Friends had brought against them for perjury. Later they put in a demurrer against the*

Friends' plea, arguing that the court was competent to deal with the former indictment, but the hearing of the demurrer was deferred until the next sessions.

Six months later Thomas Moseley, Thomas Beard, Mary Akehurst, widow, and Mary Akehurst, spinster, Thomas Robinson and his wife, and Thomas Akehurst were sent before Sir John Stapley, Justice, on the information of John Eresby, priest, that they had absented themselves from church on three Sundays. They pleaded that they had been convicted before and were thus not liable to be prosecuted again for the same offences, yet Sir John Stapley issued a warrant to levy three shillings each on their goods. As some did not have goods to be distrained, the Justice, arguing that a warrant levied on all had to be satisfied by all, issued a further warrant to imprison all of the defendants, but the constable did not execute it.

On the 16th of the 8th month, 1683, Ambrose Galloway, junior, was presented at the Bishop's Court, by John Eresby, priest of the parish of All Saints, for not going to the parish church to hear divine service, and for not receiving the Sacrament according to church law. Ambrose appeared and alleged that:-
- it had been proved that the priest had foresworn himself
- the priest had never told him that it was his duty to go
- the priest should have more time to convince him of this
- that he was already convicted of this offence and having been sentenced to a continuing punishment should not be punished twice for the same offence and other arguments which he had put into writing.

It is likely that these defences were prepared on the advice of Meeting for Sufferings which had circulated legal advice to many meetings. He was allowed time to bring a certificate of his former conviction, and this absolved him from further punishment on account of not attending church. Since this was his first prosecution for not receiving the Sacrament he was admonished to receive the Sacrament at Easter next. He was later brought to court for not having done so, but pleaded successfully that he could not do so as he was in prison at the time. He was discharged, but ordered to receive it at the next Whitsunday. After failing to do so he pleaded that receiving the Sacrament would have been against the law as he had not been baptised. This was accepted, but he was admonished to learn the Catechism and be baptised before Michaelmas. Nevertheless, he was excommunicated immediately. Although it might appear that excommunication was just what he wanted, Ambrose would have also lost valuable civil rights.

On the 5th day of the 2nd month, 1684, Ambrose Galloway, senior, Ambrose Galloway, junior, Richard Stephens, Benjamin Moseley, all of Lewes, Nicholas Beard, senior, and Nicholas Beard, junior, of Rottingdean, were all arrested and kept close prisoners at the White Horse Inn until the 10th of the month because they would not *promise to appear at the sessions.* When the bailiffs brought them before the sessions the prisoners were freed and the bailiffs were denied their expenses.

The Friends indicted the previous year were recalled and there were further arguments about their liability under the Statute of the 35th of Queen Elizabeth. they argued that if they were found guilty and would not abjure their offence would be a capital one which was beyond the jurisdiction of the Quarter Sessions. The Justices left the matter until they could seek the opinion of the Judges and at the next Assizes held at East Grinstead Judges Carleton and Pemberton gave their opinion that the matter was not one for Quarter Sessions, and Friends were not called again.

On the first day of the 4th month 1684 the excommunication of Richard Stephens was published for the non-payment of four shillings and 6 pence towards the repairs of the church of St Michael. A neighbour paid the money on his behalf but the write of excommunication was taken against him by Walter Willard and Thomas Verall the wardens and Benjamin Henshaw a proctor of the same parish. On this writ he was taken by Richard Browne, a bailiff, to the common gaol at Horsham where he was detained until the 22nd day of the first month 1685/6 when he was discharged by the Declaration of Liberty by King James the Second. A further warrant for a sum of twenty pounds, for not going to church, was taken out against him. The Sheriff was empowered to secure costs of 140 pounds but the process was not executed.

Friends were not strangers to Horsham Gaol. For a while they paid the gaoler a small sum to keep a room there for them and to provide it with fresh straw until the justices heard of the practice and brought it to an end, sending Richard Luckins, the gaoler, to the House of Correction in Lewes for three weeks. *The Crime that was layd to his Charg beeing only that he had given more Liberty to the people Called Quakers (who were then in his keeping) than they were willing they should have had, a very Remarkable Cruelty.*

Mary Akehurst was one of the last prisoners there. It is recorded above that John Eresby's accusation against her son Thomas was proved false and Eresby was indicted for perjury. Friends assumed that it was from motives of revenge that Eresby sued her for tithes and excommunicated her for refusing to pay. On Sunday morning, 10th July 1687, although poor and weak, she was taken on horseback to *Horsham Gaol, one of the bailiffs drunk with many oaths threatening that if she could not hold on he would have her dragged at the horse's tail.* Eventually they got her to the gaol where she remained a close prisoner for 7 months and was afterwards committed to the Kings Bench prison in London.

The Kings Bench prison was for debtors. It is not surprising that Friends who had been fined and had the tools of their trade taken from them should find themselves unable to pay their creditors, but it is surprising that they counted it a kindness when one of these creditors sued them. The debtor's prison was a much more comfortable place than Horsham Gaol!

Soon afterwards in 1689 the Act of Toleration released Friends from the obligation of attending church and taking the sacraments. This ended the worst of the persecution, but they were still liable for the payment of tithes and suffered much financial loss during the next two centuries.

One remaining source of friction with the community was the refusal of Friends to celebrate religious festivals. On the 25th day of the 10th month [of the old calendar] *1689, called Christmas, the shop window of Richard Stephens being open a at other times, came James Browne, a tinker, with a rabble of other loose persons, pretending orders from the Constables of the town, William Read and James Bridger, and beat and broke down his windows, broke an iron wire grate and spoiled much of his goods; whereupon he went and made complaint to Henry Pelham (Justice, so called), who told him that he might have kept his shop shut.*

Richard Stephens was also much abused by the rabble in the street the third and fourth day of the month, called the 'fast days', by throwing down his windows and damaging his goods. Many other Friends suffered in the same way. On the 14th day of the 12th month 1688 the thanksgiving day for the Prince of Orange, Benjamin Moseley's shop windows were open and his goods set out as usual, although he was not at home. Walter Rowe the younger and one Kennard and many more of the rabble came with them and they threw his goods in the street and dirt and broke his iron grate and threw down his windows and nailed some of them up.

Friends were also penalised for their refusal to enlist or pay for the militia. The 11th day of the 5th month 1690 Major Monk came with his troop of soldiers assisted by William Read and James Bridger, constables, and Robert Collgeat, headborough, to search the house of Ambrose Galloway for arms, and finding none they demanded and seized his horse which was at pasture close by. The Major ordered his soldiers to take him to the Star Inn [now the Town Hall] *taking from him a new boot (the fellow of it not being at home) and a fowling piece which they carried to the Turk's Head* [on the corner of Albion Street and School Hill] *where the Deputy Lieutenants at that time were sitting. Ambrose Galloway appeared before them demanding his goods. After many disputes and words used to entangle him about the lawfulness of the government and the rights of King James and King William, Ambrose, alleging them to be matters which did not concern him, nobody accused him of anything relating thereto, nor had found any cause of suspicion of his disturbing the government. After about 3 hours he had his goods returned.*

He had refused to pay about seven shillings, a part of a musket [the cost of maintaining a soldier] charged on him by Captain Walter Dobell's company. The same day William Read and James Bridger, constables, and Robert Collgeat and John Walter, headboroughs, by warrant from the deputy Lieutenants took from him fourteen pewter plates, ten large pewter dishes, a pair of brass candlesticks, a pewter basin, six pewter porringers, a pewter still and other goods to the value in all of about five pounds. About two weeks later Robert Collgeat the headborough returned everything except the fourteen pewter plates which they had sold. Ambrose had no notice that he was charged with any part of a soldier until the night before, and no money had been demanded previously, but he was told that he must defend himself immediately.

Respectability

George Fox wrote in his journal:-
At the first convincement when Friends could not put off their hats to people, nor say you to a particular, but thee and thou; and could not bow, nor use the world's salutations nor fashions nor customs – and many Friends being tradesmen of several sorts – they lost their custom at the first, for the people could not trade with them nor trust them. And for a time people that were tradesmen could hardly get money to buy bread, but afterwards when people came to see Friends' honesty and truthfulness and yea and nay at a word in their dealing, and their lives and conversations did preach and reach to the witness of God in all people, and they knew and saw that they would not cozen and cheat them for conscience' sake towards God:- and that at last they might send any child and be as well used as themselves at any of their shops, so then the things altered so that the inquiry was where a draper or shopkeeper or tailor or shoemaker or any other tradesman that was a Quaker: then that was all their cry, insomuch that Friends had double the trade beyond all of their neighbours: and if there was any trading they had it.

Nevertheless the period 1690 to 1760 was in many ways one of decline. As the first generation of Friends passed away the Meeting increasingly consisted of birth-right members rather than those converted by a life-changing experience. John Stephenson Rowntree wrote in 1859 of the period as one of the *'diminished effusion of the Holy Spirit'*, while William Braithwaite considered that the Society *'established a strong organisation and lost something of its soul.'*

At first there was no formal membership – Quakers were defined as those who regularly attended Meeting for Worship – but some problems made a clearer definition necessary. Each Monthly Meeting helped any Friend in need so that no Friend had to rely on parish relief. Every application for help was examined by the Meeting, and while no Friend was allowed to suffer real want, neither was idleness indulged or any extravagance tolerated. In 1712 the Meeting considered the case of Thomas Rowland whose family had been assisted for some time. It was reported that they had more and better goods than seemed appropriate, and visitors were appointed to inspect the house. Very little was found that could be spared except a pair of wheels, an old plough and some husbandry tackle. These were sold, to recover in part the money which monthly Meeting had spent on two pounds worth of wheat.

Eligibility for relief depended on membership, and the procedure for joining was increasingly clearly defined. By the end of the century any new convert could apply to Monthly Meeting, or Monthly Meeting itself would take the initiative, and visitors were appointed to meet with the applicant and report back. The children of Friends were automatically members. Thus people were either 'birthright' Quakers, or they became members by 'convincement'.

From the beginning there was a need for discipline. Surrounded by other sects, such as the Ranters, whose message licensed immorality, it was necessary for Friends to witness to their Inward Light by the innocence of their conduct. [Friends today often speak of the 'Inner Light', but the phrase used in the early days was 'the Inward Light of Christ'] They knew that their opponents were ready to publicise any difference between their profession and practice. Friends whose conduct was inconsistent with Quaker morality (disorderly walkers) were first reproved privately, then publicly, if necessary, and finally, if they did not respond, they were disowned. Any Friends whose actions had brought the Society into public disrepute, but who had repented, were required to publish papers of condemnation of their acts. Those who would not or could not conform again to the testimonies of the Society were disowned. The Book of Disownments makes both sad and tedious reading. Friends could be disowned for abandoning the Society or behaving immorally, paying tithes, employing a substitute in the militia, marrying out or bankruptcy. Bankruptcy may have been a misfortune, but Friends were considered at fault if they entered into any commitment which they could not absolutely guarantee to fulfil.

By far the most common reason for disownment was marrying out. The determination of early Friends to avoid the 'hireling priests' forced them to establish their own marriage ceremony and this received legal approval almost immediately, but it was only legal when both parties were Quakers. Marriage out was penalised because it had recognised the authority of an Anglican priest. Friends had limited opportunities to meet prospective marriage partners within the Society, so many married out. The marriage of first cousins was prohibited by Quaker rules, but not by the laws of the land, so others left to marry in church. Those who remained were less likely to marry than outsiders, and those who did marry created a complex network of intermarried families.

Disownment was in many ways not as harsh as it may sound. Those who were disowned were free to continue attending Meeting for Worship, and many did so, but they were not allowed to take part in business meetings or to give money to the Society. The law gradually made allowances for Quaker peculiarities, but such concessions as being allowed to affirm rather than give evidence on oath were not open to the disowned, many of whom still retained their Quaker tenderness of conscience about such matters.

Tradition had replaced an adventurous response to the Inward Light. The 'plain dress' of the original Friends remained unchanged, but the nature of the Testimony was subtly different. The simple, practical clothes of one generation became a uniform for subsequent ones and the obligation to take on the uniform when joining the Society created a barrier to membership. They refused 'hat honour' and insisted on referring to one person as 'thee' rather than 'you'. Originally such behaviour was regarded as highly offensive to a population for whom the niceties of social distinction were important, but eventually it became merely quaint – a Quaker mannerism. Even more harmful was the testimony against art, music and literature.

In other ways, Quaker distinctiveness had its advantages. Most Friends had no time for the predominantly classical education of the day, they were not eligible to attend the universities, and the Test Acts disqualified them from most public offices. This restricted them to fields in which they excelled, business and science.

It was about the year 1700 that the Rickman family came to Lewes. They may have been related to the Rickmans at Arundel who had suffered in the persecutions. During the next century and a half they, their relatives and their employees dominated Lewes Meeting. Dates of birth and death are given after many of the name quoted later in an attempt to distinguish between different people with identical names. The habit of giving the eldest boy the first name of his father or grandfather adds to the confusion. In an age of high infant mortality it was common to use the same name for successive children until one survived to carry on the tradition.

John Rickman (1715-1789) who married Elizabeth Peters is one of the first of the dynasty in Lewes. He was a brewer and the freeholder of the Bear Inn in the Cliffe, immediately to the East of Cliffe Bridge. At that time the Cliffe was not part of Lewes proper, and the Bear Inn was in practice the Town Hall, as well as the centre of the Lewes wool trade. Quakers then had no objection to alcoholic drinks, apart from spirits, although they actively discouraged drunkenness. Nevertheless some very unquakerly activities took place there. In *1775 the celebrated midget, Margaret Morgan, who stands only 31 inches high at the age of 17 years* was exhibited, and in 1780 there was a performance of the Beggar's Opera.

His eldest son, Richard Peters Rickman (1745-1801) succeeded him, and appears in the records not merely as inn-keeper and brewer, but also as banker. Richard is one of the few who 'married out' and not merely escaped being disowned, but eventually became one of the key figures in the meeting. Friends were usually aware of any courtship taking place, and warned those likely to *marry one not of our persuasion* against taking such a step. A Friend who persisted in this was so clearly setting himself against the meeting that disownment was inevitable. On 5th June 1767 he married Mary Verrall (1749-1818) in Cliffe Church. Friends were apparently not expecting this, since there is no minute of Friends appointed to visit him, but a minute dated 14th June 1767 reads:

Whereas Richard Peters Rickman by misconduct hath incurred the censure of this Meeting, this Meeting appoints John Snashall and Daniel Burns to Treat with him and make their report to the next Monthly Meeting. Further visits were paid to him, and in April 1768 he sent to the Meeting a Letter of Condemnation for his Past Crimes and misconduct' The Lewes Minutes usually distinguish between breaches of the rules of the Society and 'crimes', so the use of the word 'crime' here may be significant. The reported birth of a son in 1767 suggests that there was a reason for the hasty marriage. *In May 1768 the Friends appointed to wait on Richard Peters Rickman having given a satisfactory account of his behaviour which together with his Steady and Consistent deportment and also his paper of Condemnation, Friends hath restored him in fellowship and Communion and he is himself reinstated as a Member of our Society.*

The youngest son of John Rickman was Thomas 'Clio' Rickman (1760-1834). As a boy he spent time in the company of Tom Paine who lived in Lewes from 1768 to 1774, a friendship which cannot have been welcomed by Friends. When the Meeting had *reason to apprehend that 'he had the intention of marriage with a person not of our society'* they warned him against any process of this nature, but he married in Cliffe Church in 1783 and was disowned soon afterwards.

Lower writes of him in *The Worthies of Sussex*: *He lived for many years in Marylebone Street, London, where he carried on the trade of bookseller. He published two volumes of poems besides occasional pieces. His habits, manners and personal appearance were very peculiar, and it has been said that he was the original from which the well known comic-character of 'Paul Pry' was drawn. His verses never surpass mediocrity, and often descend to bathos.* His lasting work is his biography of Tom

Paine, but even this bears the marks of his eccentricity. The end-papers advertise his other works, including *The Atrocities of a Convent in three volumes*, and describe a patent signal trumpet which he had invented. We know from a newspaper advertisement that his works could be bought in Lewes from Miss Rickman's bookshop near the bridge.

Impromptu
to
THOMAS PAINE.
At Paris, July 1802.

Franklin, your old and faithful friend,
Who wit and truth did always blend;
With energy would oft' declare,
"Where freedom is, my country's there"

And you as oft' would make reply,
while genius sparkled in your eye,
(That eye, where wit and judgement keen,
And brilliant intellect are seen)

"Where freedom is not, that's my land,
"And there I'll live, and make a stand
Against what tyranny has plann'd."

By this good rule, my friends I vow,
Your station is most proper now;
Nor need you any further dance,
Indeed you're quite at home in France.

'Clio' Rickman

    Tom Paine was not a Quaker, but as some books dealing with his time in Lewes are in error about his Quaker connections, some clarification may be in order. His father was a Quaker, and his mother an Anglican. There is no record of his attending Quaker meetings while at Lewes. Some books report that Samuel Ollive, with whom he lodged, was a Friend, but they are not correct. Samuel Ollive attended Westgate Chapel where his son was the minister. Throughout his life Tom Paine vigorously criticised the Quakers, yet he sometimes suggested that their faith was more reasonable and closer to his beliefs than that of other denominations.

He wrote *The only people who, as a professional sect of Christians provide for the poor of their society, are people known by the name of Quakers. These men have no priests. They assemble quietly in their places of meeting, and do not disturb their neighbours with shows and noise of bells. Religion does not unite itself to show and noise. True religion is without either.*

When the National Convention in Paris debated the possible trial and execution of Louis XVI, Paine's speech was interrupted by Marat. *I deny the right of Thomas Paine to vote on such a subject; as he is a Quaker, of course his religious views run counter to the infliction of capital punishments.* It is interesting to note that Paine had the reputation of being a Quaker, and did not take the opportunity (if he had one) to correct the statement. He forcefully advanced many of the causes close to Friends, including the abolition of slavery. While his diagnosis of the causes of war is close to the Quaker point of view, he was not a pacifist.

In his will he wrote *I know not if the Society of people called Quakers admit a person to be buried in their burying ground, who does not belong to their Society, but if they do, or will admit me, I would prefer being buried there; my father belonged to that profession, and I was partly brought up in it. But if it is not consistent with their rules to do this, I desire to be buried on my own farm at New-Rochelle.* The American friends refused this on the grounds that it was not their custom to permit memorial stones, and that it was likely that his admirers would wish to raise a stone in his honour, contrary to the Society's ruling on burying grounds at that time.

Quakers have been criticised for refusing his request. Their discipline at that time forbade the erection of memorial stones. It is not clear whether the clause in the will about a head stone related only to the eventuality of his burial on the farm, or whether he would have wished for a head stone even if he was buried with the Quakers. His request was conditional on it being *consistent with their rules*, and he did not ask for any dispensation from them.

John Rickman had another son, Joseph (1749-1810), who was apprenticed to Mr Ridge, a surgeon at Lewes, and then went to Maidenhead where he practised as a druggist. Joseph's son Thomas (1776-1841) was born in Maidenhead. At the age of 18 he drew and coloured 5000 toy soldiers which he cut out and arranged in front of architectural backgrounds of military buildings. He trained as a surgeon and apothecary in London, and in 1791 he rejoined his father who had returned to Lewes, practising medicine in the Cliffe. In 1802 Thomas fell in love with his first cousin, Lucy Rickman (1772-1804). He was warned against a possible breach of the rules of the Society, but informed the visitors *that both himself and his cousin had seriously considered the matter and did not think it likely that the connection would be broken off.* They married in Cliffe Church, and when they were disowned they left Lewes.

Joseph Rickman left the Quakers and *held forth as a street preacher in most of the principal towns of the kingdom, and particularly in the metropolis, with a degree of eccentricity bordering on insanity.*

St Thomas in the Cliffe

For a while Thomas worked as a clerk in commerce and insurance, and in his spare time he studied architecture. At that time the term 'gothic' was used indiscriminately to describe any ancient building. In 1817 he published his Attempt to Distinguish the Styles of Architecture, and for this he devised the names Norman, Early English, Decorated and Perpendicular which have now passed into general use. In 1818 Parliament provided a large sum for the building of new churches, and although he had no previous practical experience the church commissioners employed him in the construction of more churches than any other architect of the time. In 1835 he returned to Lewes for the funeral of his brother John in the Friends burial ground, but as he had joined the Catholic Apostolic Church he was no longer acceptable to his old Quaker friends.

The minute books of the 18th century are, on the whole, remarkable for their lack of variety. The most common entry is a list of the names of Friends attending, a note that the meeting was held *in a good degree of love and unity*, followed by announcement of the place of the next meeting. The more spectacular events such as disownments stand out from these modest statements so much by contrast that it is easy to be totally mistaken about the proportions of one to the other. The following extracts from the Woman Friends Monthly Meeting minute book are from the period 1767-1784, but could have been drawn from any time in that century. Although men's and women's meetings were both conducted in a business-like manner, the records reveal that the women clerks were far less literate than the men.

At a monthly meeting held at Gardener's Street the 13th of the 11th month 1768 were present – Sarah Rickman, Aley Rickman, Sarah Winton.

John Horne and Sarah Rickman laid their intentions of marriage before this Meeting. Two friends, viz Rebecca Rickman and Aley Rickman were appointed to inquire into the Clearness of Sarah Rickman, agreeable to the good order established. (Gardner Street is now part of Herstmonceux)

At a monthly meeting held at Lewes the 11th of the 12th month 1768 were present – Ann Rickman, Ann Burns, Margaret Shaw and several others.

Samuel Rickman reported the results of the inquiry respecting Sarah Rickman's clearness, which was, that the Friends appointed found her clear of all others, and free to pursue her intentions, consistent with the order among Friends, so she appeared with John Horne, and they both declared their mind to be same as at last meeting relative to their purposed marriage.

Our next Monthly Meeting to be held at Brighthelmstone if the Lord permit.

At a Monthly Meeting of women Friends Brighthelmstone the 9th of the 1st month 1780:
There was present
of Brighthelmstone - Jane Mitchell, Tabitha Hilton, Elizth Likeman, Mary Osborn,
  Mary Mitchell
of Lewes - Mary Rickman younger, Ann Rickman, Mary Rickrnan elder
of Herstmonseux - none.

Mary Rickman elder reports her delivering the money collected at Last Meeting 1 pound, 11 shillings to the Quarterly meeting and that the Friends of Arundel and Chichester was wrote to desiring them to double their collections for next quarter also a verbal message was sent to the Friends of Horsham and Ifield. Letting them know the Friends of Brighthelmstone, Herstmonseux and Lewes have doubled theirs this last quarter as it was proposed the proceeding quarter held at Horsham - also that the Quarterly Meeting was held at Lewes in a good degree of love and unity - our ensuing Monthly Meeting to be held at Lewes if the Lord permits.

At a monthly meeting of Women friends held at Lewes the 7th of the 12th month 1783.

There was present
of Lewes - Ann Burns Elizth Rickman Susanna Cruttenden Mary Rickman Elizth Newnham Elizth Martin Mary Rickman
of Barcomb and several others
of Brighthelmstone - Jane Mitchell Sarah Glaisyer
of Herstmonceux - None

Our Friends Elizth Martin and Mary Rickman appointed to attend the Ensuing Quarterly Meeting of Woman Friends of Arundel.

This meeting appointed our Friends Elizth Rickman and Susanna Cruttenden to visit Mary Grantham - a person who has attended Friends meetings several years and appears of a sober orderly conversation - and report to our next monthly meeting whither they find her desirous of becoming a member of our Society.

We also collected at this time and paid a bill for cleaning, etc to the Meeting house.

	s	d
Thirteen shillings and four pence	13	4
and five shillings to the woman	5	0
for taking care of the key		

At a Monthly Meeting of Women Friends held the 8th of the 2d month 1784.

The old meeting House was thought unfit. Therefore Friends adjourn till next month.

At a Monthly Meeting of women Friends the 14th of the 3rd month 1784
There was present
of Lewes – Ann Burns Elizabeth Rickman Susanna Cruttenden
     Elizabeth Martin Mary Rickman Elizabeth Newnham and
     Mary Rickman of Barcombe

Brighthelmstone – Jane Coates and Sarah Glaisyer
Herstmonceux – None

The friends appointed to visit Mary Grantham report they did visit her and found her desirous of becoming a member of our Society and there being no objection Friends receive her as such.

There was collected at this time 7 shillings - 4 of which was sent to the woman who cleaned the old meeting house and 3 was sent to the other woman who took care of the key - to pay them in full.

Quietism

By the eighteenth century the Society had moved into Quietism. Great emphasis was laid on abstaining from 'creaturely' activities, and since nothing was to be done without the complete assurance that it was the will of God, the temptation was to undertake very little in the way of new activity. It is clear that many occupied themselves with an intense religious devotion, yet the fear of speaking more than was required resulted in long meetings for worship whose almost complete silence provided little food for the less mature.

Perhaps it is not surprising that the most vivid picture of Quaker life towards the end of that period comes from a convert, William Marten (1764-1823). He was born in Barcombe and brought up in the Church of England, but went at the age of 17 to live and work with his uncle, Thomas Marten of Lewes, who was a draper and author of the book *Quakerism No Delusion*. For two years he attended the meetings of the General Baptists, and then the Calvinists for three years. After a conversion experience he rejoiced, and spent much of his time in prayer and singing, *But this was a short-lived enjoyment; for I soon found it was practised more to gratify the creature, than to exalt the great Creator.* Eventually he *attended the meetings of Friends, and also became convinced of the propriety of wearing plain apparel; of using the singular pronoun in addressing one person; and of forbearing to take off my hat by way of compliment. I was much tried with respect to this latter custom.*

At this time Friends had the practice of 'Recording Ministers'. All were bound to speak in meeting if moved to do so, but Friends who often spoke helpfully were officially recognised, and given seats on the 'stand' or 'gallery' in front of the meeting. William Marten records that *Our worthy friend and minister, Daniel Burns, of Lewes, being very ill, I felt it to be my duty to go and see him. On my entering his room, he drew a chair, that I might sit beside him: he endeavoured to speak, but was not able. After having spent about half an hour in solemn silence, I took leave of him, not expecting to see him again alive. When I had gone about forty yards from his house, a voice, which appeared to proceed from his departing spirit, addressed me thus: 'William, what shall I give thee?' I replied: "A double portion of thy good spirit." My mind then felt seasoned with good; and, from that time, I believed that it would be my lot to succeed my dear friend in the ministry.*

Some time after this, a service exceedingly trying to the creaturely part, was required of me; viz. to bear a public testimony against stage entertainments, by delivering papers, 'on the right Employment of Time', to such as might be going to the playhouse. At first I was tempted to send them by the person who distributed the play-bills; but a secret voice said: "Shall the Lord employ those in his work whom the devil employs?" I then thought of another person, but he also was rejected: I was to do it myself. The enemy, working with the flesh, suggested that I should, by such conduct, lose my business, be slighted by my relations, and called crazy; and that I might even lose my life. But I knew it to be the Lord's will and work; and was favoured with strength to deny myself, in order to obey his command. Accordingly, on the evening of the 31st of the 8th month, 1789, I stationed myself before the theatre, and distributed about 250 of the papers. A clergyman, who was about to go in, on reading the paper went away. I had also procured several printed copies of a paper, written in the form of a play-bill, and describing, in a very striking manner, 'The Great Assize, or Day of Judgment'. Some of these I caused to be posted, the next morning, opposite the theatre.

Times of national rejoicing then were celebrated by 'illuminations' - lights placed in the front windows of each house. Friends did not observe them as they were generally for military victories, and Friends mourned the loss of life on both sides. The people regarded Friends as unpatriotic and vented their fury on houses without lights. On March 11th 1789 William Marten wrote: *This night there has been a general illumination, on account of the restoration of the king's health. We had only three panes of glass broken, in consequence of not exhibiting lights; although some of our friends sustained considerable damage. I am glad that Friends stand steadfast in our testimony against the practice of illuminating, but I believe that we all sincerely rejoice at the restoration of the health of so good a king.* He commented at a later date *The English, having gained a victory at sea, over the French, the town was illuminated as a testimony of rejoicing. Oh that men would learn the religion of Jesus Christ, the Prince of Peace, then would they cease to rejoice at the destruction of their fellow-creatures.*

John Mackellow wrote in his autobiography that he was in Brighton Barracks in 1800, and began to feel that he should lay down his arms and refuse doing military duty. So he went to Lewes with a letter to William Marten's house. He was offered refreshment, but told that Marten had gone to Brighton with his wife for the day. *Soon after he came in and said that he felt constrained to come home, under an impression that something was the matter. He seemed glad to see me, and after a pause, he told me all that I had been suffering and that when the time came for me to lay down my arms, it would be in the light, and not under a cloud, and more to the same import.*

The scene from that time was wholly changed with me: I went in a state of mourning and returned rejoicing.

Daniel Burns had been 'convinced' while serving in the army, and in welcoming soldiers, William Marten was following his example. *In 1788 Burns, one of the people called Quakers, and other inhabitants of this town, rescued by their humane and public spirited interference, an unhappy private of the Eleventh Regiment of Light Dragoons, from the barbarous and persevering malignity of one of his officers. They not only exerted themselves (at considerable expense) to lay a temporary restraint on the cruelties of this military oppressor, but finally obtained the poor man's discharge by an application to the War Office.*

William Marten recorded that *it appeared to be required of me, to go to a minister of the Church of England, and advise him against being lifted up with having a large congregation, but to continue humble. I went accordingly, and he received the message in love.'* Later he wrote *'This evening took a walk with --------, a minister of the Church of England, whose conversation was edifying. I am persuaded that there are many in this establishment, both ministers and others, who are members of the church of Christ; to whom may my soul be expanded in charity.*

In 1805 he opened a first-day school for the instruction of poor children in reading and had forty to begin with. This continued until 1811, when most children were attending the Subscription School. He withdrew from business in 1817, *having been engaged therein about thirty years, and have been abundantly blessed; for although I have been diligent in my outward calling, my heart has been preserved from centering in temporal things; so that I have been enabled cheerfully to leave them all, when religious duty required.* He had other social concerns: in 1814 he collected 693 signatures for a petition against the slave trade, and he also collected £123 for 'The Retreat', the Quaker Hospital at York which pioneered humane treatment and care for the mentally ill.

He died in 1823, and his obituary in the *Sussex Weekly Advertiser* reads: *Died on Monday, the 6th instant, at his house in this town, aged 58, Mr. William Marten, one of the Society of Friends, and well known in Sussex and the neighbouring counties, as a man of eminent piety and the most diffusive benevolences, though little in his own apprehension he was in the truest sense of the word, Great in the estimation of all that knew him. His remains were interred yesterday morning in the Friend's burial ground in this town, attended by a numerous and respectable train of relatives and other sincere admirers, and also by about 500 children from the Lewes Subscription School, of which he has been one of the first promoters and most active Directors.*

1784

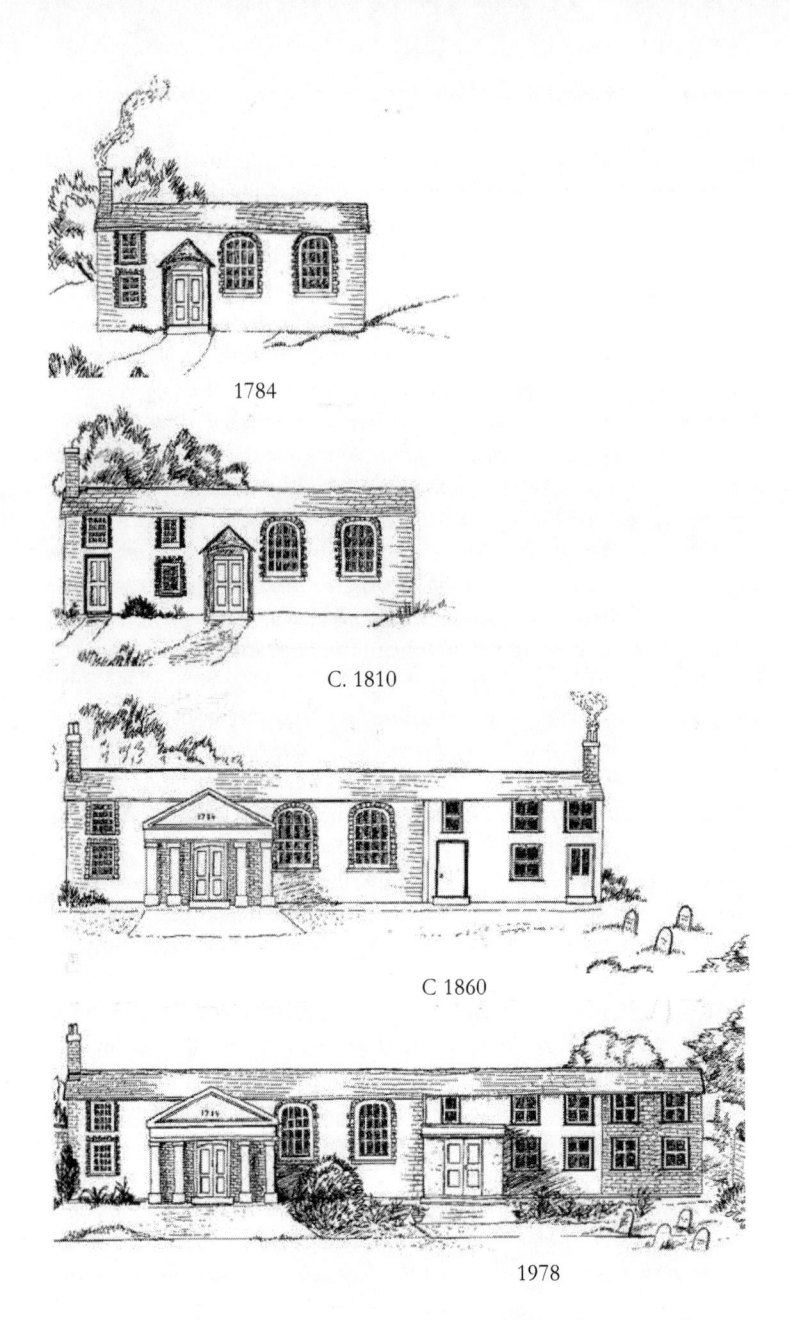

C. 1810

C 1860

1978

The meeting house as it grew from 1784 to the present day.
Drawings by Maurice Burge

The New Meeting House

The minute of 1784, above, that *the old Meeting House was thought unfit to sit in* appears near the end of a long series of reports. In November 1782 *John Rickman and Thomas Cruttenden presented a plan and estimation of charges on altering and repairing the Meeting House as requested. This meeting requests William Tuppen to join the said Friends and examine the estimation making alteration in the plan as seems necessary to them and report their proceedings to the next sitting of this meeting.* This was for extending the building in length for the better accommodating of Friends. *In January 1783 William Tuppen with the Friends appointed have re-examined the Meeting House at Lewes as requested and find the method will be to take off the roof and prepare two convenient chambers on the second floor, which they apprehend will cost nearly ninety pounds.*

In July the matter was still under discussion. *This meeting considered the considerable expense that will attend repairing the meeting house at Lewes, and other disagreeable circumstances propose building another at a more convenient place; or repair the present house which is now left to the following Friends to proceed therein [eight names given]. Next month Thomas Marten and Thomas Cruttenden junior two of the Friends appointed to proceed in repairing the Meeting House at Lewes or build a new one as they judge most expedient report they are not come to a final conclusion which report this Meeting expects more fully at our next.*

In September The committee appointed to repair the Meeting House at Lewes or to build a new Meeting House and dwelling House adjoining thereto requests Thomas Rickman, senior, to apply to the Quarterly Meeting for their approbation to sell the present Meeting House at Lewes when a suitable purchaser offers and the money arising therefrom to go towards building a new house with dwelling house adjoining there to.

Our reasons for this application are these: near the present Meeting House is a slaughter house and the soil arising therefrom is sometimes thrown out in the road leading to the house which in summer season is very offensive, and lately a turner's workshop is erected adjoining the meeting house. Frequently the turner's lathe is going on the weekday which is disturbing to the Meeting when sitting. The intended new Meeting House and dwelling house we propose will cost near £220 and the money arising from the sale of the present house we apprehend may be about £100, the difference we hope to raise by subscriptions in the compass of Lewes Monthly Meeting.

In October, with the approval of Quarterly Meeting, the meeting appointed Thomas Cruttenden, Thomas Martin, Thomas Rickman, junior, to make sale of the present Meeting House and to be delivered to the purchaser by the 4th month

1784. We are of the opinion the price ought not to be less than £105, but more if it can be obtained.

By November a purchaser had been found, to pay £110 when the building was vacated. The building was sold to the Particular Baptists. There had been a dispute at their chapel on Chapel Hill, which resulted in some of them being locked out of their building, and they were in urgent need of an alternative. Within a short while they took land in Foundry Lane, on lease from Richard Peters Rickman, and built a new chapel. The existence of the deed and their temporary occupation of the old Quaker Meeting House resulted in a long-held belief that the original Friends Meeting House was in Foundry Lane, but W. K. Rector finally rediscovered the true situation when he was able to locate the building from Thomas Woollgar's book *Spicilegia*. This identification can be confirmed by noting that legal proceedings against the owner of the meeting house were initiated by the Lewes and not the Cliffe authorities.

The work was complete by the 13th of June, 1784 when Thomas Cruttenden brought in a report:
Sale of late Meeting House £110. 0. 0 Subscriptions 121. 6. 0
The subscribers were Thomas Rickman, senior and Thomas Rickman junior, £21 each; Daniel Burns, Thomas Cruttenden, Thomas Marten, John Rickman, Richard Peters Rickman, Samuel Rickman senior, Mary Rickman (Barcombe), 10 guineas each; Christopher Spencer, 5 guineas and Samand Carter, 1 guinea.
[The total in the minute book is in error by 10 shillings.]

Paid George Whyles	
as per contract	£188. 5. 0
Extra work	27.19.1
Thos. Boxall, bricklayer	7. 7. 6
George Verrall, making of seats	1. 6. 8
2 Bath stones	1. 4. 0
Painting	1.14.9
John Hardiman	1. 1. 0
Sundry disbursements	10.6
	229. 8. 6
Balance for future disbts.	£ 2. 7. 6

The completion was celebrated, at raising day, by a dinner at a cost of £1.11.6d. The building, above the foundation walls, was timber framed, and the front facing was in mathematical tiles. Lewes Meeting House, with the exception of King's Lynn, is the only one in the South to have had a timber porch.

The interior of the meeting room was much as it is now. The benches would have faced forward, with a gangway down the centre. Men would have sat on one side, nearer the door, and women on the other. At the front was a low platform, the 'stand' or 'ministers gallery'. Men and women ministers sat facing the others, and the other weighty members had the front seat below the stand.

The Meeting Room as it may have appeared in the mid-nineteenth century
Drawing by Maurice Burge

There were two stoves, on stone slabs which were visible until renovations in 1987. There would have been little provision for artificial lighting, as meetings always took place in daylight hours. The gallery proper, at the back, could be divided off from the meeting room by sliding shutters. A guide-book to Lewes written in 1824 estimates the capacity of the room as 150 persons, probably including the gallery, but in 1851 the capacity was stated as 105 persons, with the gallery not counted in the space used for public worship. The men retired to the gallery for their business meetings, which were separate from the women's. Beneath the gallery were the rooms occupied by the caretaker.

When Thomas Scattergood visited the meeting on Sunday 25th February 1789 he was not impressed. He had been born in New Jersey in 1748. *As a young man he yielded to the corrupt inclinations of the vain mind, indulging in folly and forming associations, the tendency of which was to alienate him from a serious and self-denying life.* Although later he was troubled by an incident when, as a schoolboy, he stole apples, it seems that the worst that he did was to indulge in sailing on the Delaware river on Sunday afternoons. After some years of trying to resist the call he devoted himself to the ministry. His tender conscience and willingness to confront others with what he considered as their failings now makes him appear an unattractive character, but it seems that he was much loved and admired in his day. Eventually he came to England where he remained for 6 years.

At Lewes Meeting he was disappointed to find that there was no afternoon meeting, and that they were holding Preparative Meeting on the First-day, rather than a weekday. He felt that he should stay, but couldn't find words to express his unease. He decided to take charge of the proceedings, and suggested that men and women should sit together, although they generally held their business meetings separately, and he proposed that they should read the queries which at this time were answered in writing and forwarded to Quarterly Meeting. All went well until the questions on plainness. Friends were expected not merely to wear plain dress - the Quaker uniform - but also to keep to plainness of speech, referring to days and months by number rather than by the 'heathen' names, and to address individuals as 'thou' or 'thee' rather than 'you'.

In a well-ordered meeting the answer about plainness of speech, behaviour and apparel, as an example to children and servants, should have been a simple 'Yes', but truth required Lewes Friends to qualify this. Thomas Scattergood wrote that *one or two whose appearance did not strike me as pleasant, even to the outward eye, proposed that it should be more full, and say, generally careful. I felt much on this occasion, and indeed before, and had to query who there was among them that looked like Friends, with more of a very close nature.*

On the following day he visited several Friends, and with each of them he had 'opportunities' (to speak to them privately about their spiritual state). *At one Friend's home much ignorance and rawness appeared; but I was enjoined to be tender.* Another Friend told him that she felt 'comfortable', whereupon he replied that *he wished that it were otherwise; for how could any rightly concerned Friend feel comfortable, when the walls and gates of Zion were laid waste, as in this place.*

By 1801 some alterations were necessary. In January 1802 John Godlee brought in sundry bills amounting to £69.11s.4d which he has discharged leaving a balance due to him of £2.7.4.1. Nevertheless more needed to be done. When, in November, the additional work was completed bills, said to be for £44.15.0, were delivered to William Marten and John Rickman. They found a few trifling errors which reduced them to £44.8.21, but the subscriptions at that time amounted to only £31.15.6, and John Godlee was directed to pay the balance from Monthly Meeting funds.

At present we do not know what these alterations were, but examination of the back of the meeting room gives us some clues. The original doors are now permanently closed, and the door from the porch obviously replaced them. The old porch was rebuilt and is now more than twice its original width. From the edge of the old door to the other side of the room the long floor boards came to an end, and the last few feet at the back were boarded separately. The panels on the wall at the back are a little incongruous (even before the door on the west wall was opened, last century, and then later closed off). The gallery once came further forward, but it was moved back to make the meeting room proper a little larger. This adaptation isn't entirely successful; the stairs were originally at the back of the gallery, but now the stairwell comes between the gallery and the meeting room.

John Godlee, who was known in the town as a respected tradesman, and who appears in the records of the Meeting for many years as a capable administrator, had a colourful life before coming to Lewes. He was born in 1762 in Ratcliffe Highway, Wapping, near the house of Captain James Cook. At the age of fourteen he was bound apprentice, as a cabin boy to Captain Charles Pea, and he spent the next nine years at sea, shipwrecked several times, once wintering with native Americans. He was often armed, carrying a cutlass and two pistols, one of which misfired and left him with a permanently contracted hand. His ship carried horses for the British Army which was fighting the American War of Independence, and his ship carried 'Letters of Marque', permitting it to capture enemy vessels. Mistakenly his ship captured a ship which belonged to Guernsey, and only quick apologies saved them from the capital charge of piracy. Passing through the Labrador Straits he fell from the topmast. A sailor who saw him tied a rope around himself and jumped in, and John Godlee was hauled back on deck. He was not pleased when peace with America was proclaimed, because his wages were reduced one half, and he left the sea, to his father's great annoyance. Some of the members of the family had been Quakers, but it appears that they did not continue in membership as they commanded armed vessels. It was perhaps through a memory of this family link that John Godlee started attending Friends meetings. He worked as a clerk in London, until one of his fellow-clerks introduced him to Thomas Harben of Lewes, and it was there that he met the Rickman family, joined Lewes Meeting, and worked for the Rickman family for ten years until he was taken into partnership just before marrying Mary Rickman. He managed the Rickman business for many years, but later became a banker and importer, especially of coal. Many years later, when in Bear Yard, by chance he met the sailor who had rescued him.

The Early 19th Century

The Meeting still had its problems, and the following extracts from the minutes of the Women's Meeting reveal that the discipline and breaches of it had changed very little during the preceding century.

In 1802, *This meeting, being informed that contrary to the repeated advice of friends, Jane Coates is married to a person not of our society, appoints William Robert Twiner and John Glaisyer senior in conjunction with the women friends, either to visit her or to draw up a testimony of disownment against her as way may open.*

At the next meeting: *The following testimony of disownment of Jane Williams late Coates was brought to the meeting, which being twice read, was agreed to, and sent to the woman's meeting. William Robert Twiner is desired to hand her a copy thereof to present to her:*
Whereas Jane Williams late Coates, a member of this meeting, after repeated admonitions hath married in a manner contrary to the rules of our society, whereby she disunites herself as a member therefore, and in conformity to the good order established among us we give forth this our testimony, that she is no longer a member in unity with us.
Nevertheless we retain a tender regard for her wellbeing, here and hereafter, with desires that she may be favoured to stand open to the true teacher within, Christ Jesus the Light of Life, and sink down in resignation to His will, as clay in the hands of the Potter that He may form and fashion her to His praise and her everlasting peace.

There was a different problem with Mary Osborn of Brighton. She had attended the meeting for more than twenty years, and as one sometimes appointed to attend Monthly Meeting she had no excuse for not knowing the discipline. The meeting was *informed that Mary Osborn has been in the practice of intemperance in drinking, and appoints two women friends to visit her thereon and requests the men friends assistance therein.*

The result was unfavourable: William Marten and John Glaisyer report that *they in company with one of the women friends appointed have visited Mary Osborne and found her so far from that sensible and penitent state that was desirable that they are afraid another visit will not be attended with any good effect. They are therefore requested to draw up a testimony of disownment against her and present it at a future meeting.*

Matthew Bourne Likeman was a cause for concern *respecting his absconding from his apprenticeship & entering on board a ship of war.* John

Glaisyer, William Tuppen and William Marten were appointed to keep him under their care.

It must have been a great source of distress to Christopher Spencer senior that: *This meeting, being informed that Christopher Spencer junior has been guilty of great immorality in his conduct so as to bring reproach on our Religious Society, appoints Willm Tuppen and Willm Marten to visit him and report. Next month they reported that they have visited Christopher Spencer Jun and find the report respecting him to be true, namely, that a young woman is with child by him and that, as he did not seem sufficiently contrite for the sin, they thought it would be right for friends to testify their abhorrence of such a crime by disowning him, which being also the judgement of this meeting, we appoint the said William Marten and William Tuppen to draw up a testimony of disownment against him and bring to the next meeting.*

It is from diaries like those of William Marten, quoted in a previous chapter, that we learn something of the quieter, spiritual life of the Society. His obituary, in a secular newspaper, was very different from those published by Friends. From 1813 onwards *The Annual Monitor* was published. originally a pocket book with notes of a few friends who had died in the preceding year it became, in practice, the official obituary for all Friends in Britain. The entry for William Marten simply reads:

William Marten 58. 6th 1st mo. 1823 Lewis.

He was a minister, and much beloved by his friends and neighbours.

The cryptic entries of the first volumes eventually gave way to long essays. The early ones are remarkable for summarising the work of a lifetime in a few lines, while recording a breath by breath account of the last few hours. This emphasis was inevitable as the Book of Discipline at the time required Friends to be certain that the last words of dying members were carefully recorded. It is a shock to read Quaker theological or devotional works of the time, since they appear to have much more in common with modern fundamentalists than with modern Friends. It may be even harder to accept that the pious, other-worldly attitudes were not a momentary aberration, but were the mainstream of the Society's thought and worship for nearly two centuries. There are no detailed obituaries of members of Lewes Meeting in the early 1800's, but the pathetic testimony to Sarah Lidbetter who died in 1831 at the age of nine would accurately reflect their attitudes and beliefs. The Lidbetter family attended Brighton Meeting but they lived at Southwick.

Daughter of Bridger and Elizabeth Lidbetter. She was from a very little child fond of reading the Holy Scriptures, and other religious books. She also enjoyed attending our meetings for worship; and very early experienced the comfort and advantage of secret prayer. She was obedient, obliging and affectionate to her parents, of steady carriage and behaviour; and although much hidden, being a child of few words, she was much beloved and respected by all who knew her; and her mother says: "I never remember her to have needed correction; but when at any time she detected herself in error, her sorrow and grief were such as to need all the comfort and consolation I could give."

About three weeks before her death, she had her sister, her little brother, and two orphan cousins who lived with them, around her bed, to each of which she gave much suitable counsel. She also imparted suitable advice to those who attended her in her protracted illness, often expressing in grateful terms her acknowledgement of their kindness. Sometimes in the night when she had sharp spasms in her side, so that the perspiration ran down her face, she said with a sweet smile: "Mother, how these pains remind me of the suffering of my dear Saviour."

After this she enjoyed some hours of calm; and smiling said: "Now I seem not to mind pain; and, though sharp, can rejoice in the midst of it; I feel so sure it will be well with me, and so comforted in thinking that every pain makes me weaker, and brings me nearer heaven.

The day she died, she said: "Mother, I believe my breath is going; give me a sweet kiss, and send for father and uncle up stairs, that I may bid them farewell." After taking leave of her beloved mother, she dozed until within a few minutes of her close; when, agreeably to her earnest prayer, that whatever pain she might endure, she might be favoured to retain her senses to the last, she was enabled to speak with her latest breath: on awakening and her mother saying: "My dear, thou art just entering glory", she with a smile and the enquiry "Am I?" ceased to breathe.

William Marten's diary records a happier event. The following quotation incorporates some additional information from a letter (probably also the work of William Marten) addressed to John Glaisyer of Brighton, one of the founders of the present firm of Glaisyer and Kemp.

26.vi.1814. Been to Meeting this morning. This day the King of Prussia, the Emperor of Russia (Alexander I), his sister the Duchess of Oldenburg, passed through this town on their way to Dover. A great concourse of people assembled. We were at Meeting when the Emperor and his sister went through. He expressed at Portsmouth his predilection in favour of the Society of Friends and felt a strong inclination to visit a family of that persuasion on his way from Petworth to Dover to have friendly conversation for half an hour. The name of J. Glaisyer of Brighton and

- *[name omitted] of Lewes were given him, but he did not call on either. It is said he attempted it at Brighton but the crowd was so great he could not conveniently get to the house. With regard to Lewes he did not know he had passed through it, the route being intended to go by Newhaven. After he had got a little from the place, he enquired what town it was. When they got to Nathaniel Rickman's the family were standing at the gate, first-day afternoon, to see the Emperor pass. He, seeing they had the appearance of Friends, desired the driver to stop. He alighted, and asked Nathaniel Rickman if they were not of the people called Quakers.*

Being answered in the affirmative, he requested liberty to go into the house, which, of course, was most willingly granted. The Emperor offered Mary Rickman his arm and walked into the house. They were accordingly conducted into the principal apartments, the neatness of which they praised. On returning to the parlour they were invited to take some cake and wine, which they did, and seemed much pleased with the attention.

On finding that the family had not heard of the Emperor having had any communication with Friends in London, he gave them an account of his having been at meeting on a first day in Westminster, and also of the conversation he had had with some members of the Society in an interview out of meeting. They took notice of the children, and seemed unwilling to take leave, but said two or three times that they had to go as far as Dover that night, and they wished to know whether they should pass any more Friends' houses on the road. They wished to be remembered to Friends generally, said it was not likely they should ever see each other again, but they hoped they should not be forgotten.

On parting, the Emperor kissed Mary Rickman's hand, and the Duchess kissed her; they shook hands cordially with Nathaniel Rickman, saying - 'Farewell.' He behaved throughout in the most free and affable manner possible.

It appears that Nathaniel and Mary Rickman lived at Amberstone, and attended Herstmonceux meeting.

At this time members of Lewes Meeting began an association with a family which was to become famous. In 1793 Elizabeth Rickman, a cousin of Thomas Rickman the architect, married John Hodgkin (1766-1845) and moved to Pentonville, although they often visited Lewes. John taught classics and mathematics, and became famous as a calligraphist and grammarian. They had two surviving sons, Thomas (1798-1866) and John (1800-1875). Their cousin, Sarah Godlee, was the daughter of John Godlee (1762-1841, a merchant and banker in the Cliffe) and Mary Rickman Godlee. Sarah was a particularly close childhood friend of Thomas and they later fell in love. Their early correspondence, however, concerned the practical details of electrical machines:

Sarah Godlee's love to her cousin Thomas and would be much obliged to him to inform her how many gallons of electrical fluid her sister and father each received at Pentonville when last there – The reason for making this singular request is that Joseph Green, with whom she has been staying in S. Walden, said when she mentioned it that her sister had received nine gallons that he thought it was enough to cause a person's death. She thought she might be mistaken as to the quantity and deferred that matter till she could ask her cousin whom she has no doubt remembers.

The elder members of the family discouraged this relationship as the children grew into adolescence. Thomas was apprenticed to William Allen, a Quaker chemist and member of the Royal Society, but William Allen had become more interested in missionary work for Quakers, and Thomas left him. In 1817 he began a new apprenticeship with his mother's cousins, John Glaisyer and Grover Kemp who were chemists in Brighton and were very influential in Lewes Monthly Meeting. He left to study medicine and eventually became pathologist at Guy's Hospital, where he researched the condition later named after him - Hodgkin's disease.

He was very highly regarded, and for a while his sudden resignation from Guy's Hospital was a mystery. Hodgkin had for many years campaigned for the rights of aboriginal peoples, especially the American Indians. Benjamin Harrison, the Treasurer of Guy's was a Deputy Governor of the Hudson Bay Company. Hodgkin's views on the right treatment of indigenous peoples incurred Harrison's opposition, and Thomas Hodgkin no longer had any future in Guy's, nor in St Thomas's of which Harrison was also a Governor.

Sarah Godlee had married the architect John Rickman, a second cousin, and after his death in 1836 she returned to Lewes. Thomas Hodgkin had been seriously ill, and *now in his low state, with disappointment and feeble health darkening his life, he was dearer than ever to the faithful heart of cousin Sarah, and she became dearer than ever to him. She wrote his letters from his dictation: she was his devoted friend and counsellor.*

In 1840 he wrote a paper *On the Rule which Forbids the Marriage of First Cousins*, pointing out that the *Bible nowhere forbids this and often implicitly endorses it.* He also considered medical arguments against this and concluded that there was no reliable statistical evidence against it. The paper was considered, but the ruling was not changed, and it remained in force until 1883. Although Sarah may have expected

Thomas to marry her regardless of the decision, he respected the Society's authority too much, even when he believed it mistaken, and they parted in 1847 after a romance which had lasted 35 years.

Thomas's brother, John, was also interested in physical science, although they had other interests. John Stuart Mill was one of their few boyhood associates. John Hodgkin chose law as his profession, and practised very successfully as a conveyancer and teacher. He had little contact with Lewes after his early teens until he retired there in 1858, by which time he was one of the leading figures in the local meeting and the Society as a whole.

The members of Lewes Meeting in the early 18th century had included many tradesmen and shop-keepers. In 1818 John Rickman (1774-1859), the son of Richard Peters Rickman, bought Wellingham House near Ringmer and retired there. His grandson described him in terms of *unimaginative precision and tyranny*, and told of a man who had made an appointment to repay a loan of £100 at 12 noon on market day. The man was late, and John Rickman, accompanied by the young John Horne, set off in his gig for home. The debtor caught up with them on Lewes bridge, but John Rickman would have none of him. *"I can remember no appointment with anyone on Lewes bridge at five past twelve,"* he said, *"I will see thee at twelve o-clock next market day."* He then turned to John Horne and told him to work out a week's interest at five percent.

The family was no longer involved in brewing – the temperance movement was beginning to make progress among Friends – but the descendants of the earlier John Rickman continued in many lines of business including banking, corn, timber, cement, and coal. At that time Lewes was the second largest port in East Sussex, and the Rickmans and Godlees shared much of the trade. In 1839 the Sussex Express reported that:

An addition to the bustle of the river has lately been created by a number of workmen employed by Messrs. Rickman and Godlee, in the construction of a light but elegant drawbridge from warehouse to warehouse across the river.

In the same year the firm of Rickman and Godlee built their first sea-going ship in a yard just south of Cliffe Bridge, now occupied by Messrs. Chandler. The slip-way was carefully sited facing into the bend of the river. The *Lewes Castle* was a schooner 60 feet in length, and of 120 tons. Its keel was laid on Queen Victoria's coronation day.

Just west of the bridge stands Dial House. It was originally occupied by the Isteds, but by 1790 it was in the hands of Thomas

Rickman (1718-1803) who rebuilt it, extending it to one side and making it almost symmetrical. It passed to Mary Rickman (1770-1851) who married John Godlee (1762-1841). In 1826 she started a school, which her daughters Sarah and Mary Ann continued. In 1828 Sarah Godlee became the second wife of John Rickman (1780-1835). John Godlee's son, Rickman Godlee (1804-1871), eventually Sir Rickman Godlee, became an eminent lawyer and married Mary Lister, the sister of Sir Joseph Lister who pioneered antiseptic surgery. Another son of John Godlee, Burwood (1802-1882), who is described variously as gentleman, banker, land-owner and coal merchant, became one of the most prominent members of Lewes Meeting later in the century.

Later the sisters left Dial House for rooms above the subscription library in Albion Street and the house was occupied by Richard Peters Rickman (1805-1876). In 1831 he married Hannah Ashby whose sister Priscilla was married to Burwood Godlee. When *The Friars*, the Tudor mansion opposite, was demolished in 1846 they renamed Dial House in its honour.

Their son John was painfully shy. He came to Meeting, but he would slip in when everyone else had assembled, take his seat on the very last bench, and slip out again at the first sign of the end of Meeting, to avoid the agony of being spoken to, or being obliged to speak. If ever he heard company at the front door he would go out at the back and walk the two miles up the river bank to Wellingham where he would stay with his aunts until he felt sure that the visitors had gone. One day it was announced that he was to marry Ellen Bellerby who lived as companion to his aunts, and no one could imagine how he had found the courage to propose to her. It was rumoured that he had confided in his aunts, and that they helped him.

His sister, Mary Hannah was very different; sociable, gracious and charming, simple and sincere in manner. The children thought she was beautiful. She was always dressed in silks and velvet. We shall hear more of her parties in a later chapter.

Further up the High Street was a Quaker school started by Benjamin Abbott, a friend of Michael Faraday. This was Castle Place Academy, earlier occupied by Gideon Mantell. One of the specialities of the school was its instruction in printing, and copies of the school magazine have been on display in Anne of Cleves' House.

Benjamin Abbott was born at Bermondsey in 1793. His mother had been a Quaker, but had been disowned for "marrying out" and so

Benjamin did not acquire birthright membership, although he attended Quaker meetings regularly, and most of his acquaintances thought that he was a Quaker. In 1810 he started to attend lectures on science given by John Tatum and there he met Michael Faraday who at that time was apprenticed to a bookbinder, and knew no science other than what he had read in the books that he was binding. In 1812 Faraday wrote to Benjamin Abbott saying that he recognised his deficiencies in grammar and mathematics and wished to maintain a correspondence with him to improve himself. That correspondence continued until Faraday's death in 1867.

Benjamin Abbott married Eliza Aston, a Quaker, in 1831, but as he was not a member they had to marry in Stoke Newington Church and she was disowned. In 1835 they both applied for membership, and were accepted by Southwark Monthly Meeting. They moved to Lewes in 1835, where Benjamin attended Preparative Meeting regularly and was frequently one of the few representatives sent to Monthly Meeting. In 1845 they left Lewes and moved to Hitchin, where he founded Lewesford House Academy which continued until his retirement in 1858.

Jordans Meeting. Lewes would have been similar.

Modest Religion and Civic Importance

In the mid-nineteenth century Lewes Meeting was, by the standards of Quaker meetings in other parts of the country and the Lewes churches, very small. Throughout the century the number of members varied between twenty and forty, although meetings normally attracted as many attenders, some of whom were present at all meetings for worship but not for business meetings. For a century the meeting had included men of considerable status in the commercial life of the town, but socially they remained distinct from its life, and the few who achieved a national reputation did so after they left Lewes.

Almost suddenly the position changed. It was the presence of several local people of ability, the retirement to Lewes of several comparatively young men, and a readiness to participate in the life of the community that brought this about. In the last half of the century Lewes Friends held the highest offices in the Society – Clerk to Meeting for Sufferings, Assistant Clerk and Clerk to Yearly Meeting – and others who held those positions had come from Lewes or were closely related to Lewes Friends. The few Quakers from the meeting played an active part in most of the local societies, holding office in many, serving as magistrates, and one became Mayor. The long, depressing minute books of the Quietist period did no justice to the positive side of the Quaker meetings of the time, and we have little more record of the religious life of the meeting in this happier time, although many personal comments in the surviving documents make it clear that these Friends regarded worship and the affairs of ordinary life as inseparable.

From the memoirs of Friends we can build up a very detailed picture of the Meeting. The building to the north of the Meeting House dates from the late Victorian times, and from the 1970's when the old coach house was demolished, but the new work blends into the old. The Meeting House and the rooms to the south are little changed.

Opposite to the Meeting House was Leighside, the home of Burwood Godlee. Round this ran the railway. The first line, from Brighton, entered Lewes in 1846 and ran to a terminus next to Fitzroy House. Points a few hundred yards back down the line opened the track to the Hastings line, but trains which had entered the terminus had to reverse down the line to the points and then go forward up the Hastings loop. In 1847 *Two spacious platforms, one of 310 feet long on the down line and 200 feet long on the up line, have been made at the back of Mr*

Godlee's garden wall, near Pinwell, and in October of that year the London line was opened to passengers. These station arrangements have been described by one writer as 'some of the worst ever built', but they nearly resulted in a royal visit to Leighside.

In 1848 Louis Philippe, King of France, had been forced to flee his country in disguise. He landed at Newhaven, spent the night at the Bridge Hotel, and travelled to London the next day. It was expected that he would change trains at Lewes, and the principal citizens of the town were all eager to offer him hospitality. Burwood Godlee's house was the most convenient to the station, but apparently he had some scruple about meeting the king, so he and his wife Priscilla went away for the day, leaving the two maids to prepare a suitable lunch for the royal visitor. Unfortunately the railway directors commissioned a special train, and Louis Philippe passed through Lewes without stopping.

Leighside was a beautiful house in Regency style, surrounded by a veranda and set in large grounds. Around its walls were large square wooden pots containing aloes bushes, two of which reached maturity and flowered. There was a lake crossed at a narrow point by a rustic bridge and surrounded by arum lilies. Some Friends had permission to spend a while rowing before meeting. The water feeding the lake sprang up from an artesian well which he had bored, welling up through beach shingle in a rocky basin surrounded by ferns. Burwood Godlee had bought a pair of swans for the lake, but the male flew at him so viciously that he had to send it away, while the female remained, expecting to be petted and fed. One friend wrote that the silence of the meeting was sometimes broken by the scream of a peacock in a near-by garden. It would not have been out of character for Burwood Godlee to have kept peacocks! In addition to the ornamental grounds they had a walled kitchen garden with fruit, vegetables and beehives.

Leighside.
Photograph by Reeves

He was also something of an astronomer, and once invited the children of the meeting to look through his telescope at the rings of Saturn. He was a founder member of the Lewes Scientific Society, serving as a committee member for the maximum period allowed by its constitution, and then as a Vice-President for the rest of his life. He served in a similar capacity for the Mechanics Institute. Although his business and managerial talents were considerable, it was in technical matters that he excelled. At the age of twenty he was instrumental in bringing gas to Lewes, and he was chairman of the gas company 60 years later. He was a director of the Lewes Baths Association, commissioner for the town sewers, a trustee of the Lower Ouse Navigation Company, and chairman of the board of trustees of the Lewes Savings Bank. He supported the Lewes School of Art and was treasurer of the local Friends school. He served on the Board of the British Schools Association and gave £500 to the local British School in Lancaster Street and £250 to the Lewes Town Infirmary and Dispensary. In 1855 he became a county magistrate, and was the only non-conformist on the bench until the late 1870's. At the meeting he was a minister and he served as Preparative Meeting Clerk for many years.

Burwood Godlee
Photograph supplied by the Library Committee of the Religious Society of Friends

When Burwood Godlee died in December 1882 his friend Caleb Rickman Kemp wrote in his journal: *His energy was very great, concerning himself in business (both private and public) & in philanthropic works. He was very impulsive & changeable in his likes and dislikes. He was impulsive, even, in religious tenderness, and contemporaneously in severe judgement. He was very jealous of his reputation; and this, at times, led him to, unconsciously, do himself great injustice. He was a splendid man to help a friend thro' a difficulty - and had great confidence in his own opinion, tho' he was given to change his opinion somewhat quickly. In many things - including likes and dislikes - he was constant. His tastes were scientific and his highest attainments (intellectual) were scientific. Lewes has lost a patriotic inhabitant and the poor a firm friend. Many mourn his loss.*

His death spared him the heartbreak of seeing the destruction of his beloved Leighside. The Friars Walk terminus of the railway had closed in 1857, after the building of the present station. In 1868 the line was extended from the points at Pinwell out to Hamsey. This was not convenient, and in 1889 a viaduct was built through the gardens of Leighside, the arches crossing the centre of the lake. An entrance opposite All Saints led to a bridge over the railway line from which a drive descended to the house, but there was also access from a tunnel under the tracks.

In front of the meeting house was the graveyard, the older graves without headstones and the newer ones with simple headstones in a uniform style to indicate that in death all are equal. By the front wall was a row of lime trees.

Just before Meeting Friends could be seen arriving. John Rickman and his daughters drove in from Wellingham in an old fashioned family carriage called a *sociable* which opened at the back like an omnibus. Their coachman, Henry Wycherley, would put up the horse and carriage at the nearest inn, and then come to meeting. Later, perhaps because inns fell out of favour, Friends had their own coach house built. Charles Sturt drove in from East Hoathly in a pony and cart. Nathan and Rachel Smith always arrived at exactly the same time every Sunday, walking down from the High Street, *she the very pink of propriety, with her skirts lifted just so, and not a hair awry, and he, dear old man, lumbering along a few steps behind, carrying a huge umbrella.* They frowned at children who didn't sit still in Meeting, and never invited children to their home. Eliza Paine walked down from her home in Albion Street where she lived in furnished rooms. One young man came on his own. Even the children were aware that he was a Conservative: every one else was a Liberal. This was John Clay Lucas. Eventually, in 1876, he left the Meeting, was baptised an Anglican and married the daughter of a local Vicar.

The congregation was increased by about 25 girls who walked in pairs from the Quaker School in the High Street. The school had moved there from the Friars, as we shall hear later. There were also two or three girls from Caroline Speciall's school in The Crescent.

Brick paths led up to the Meeting House door and along the front of the building. Prom the porch one door opened into the small two-roomed cottage on the left, occupied by the tall old lady who looked after the premises. The other door opened into the meeting room. It was bare of any kind of ornament, even of paint. There was plain matting on the floor, and a small air-tight stove. Venetian blinds shaded the meeting in summer, and the children watched the round spots of sunshine from the cord holes creeping over the walls. The ministers' gallery was centrally placed, with two small seats on either side. In the late 1850's there were, on the woman's side (at the west) Rachel and

Matilda Rickman, while Caleb Kemp, John Hodgkin and John Rickman sat on the right. John Rickman was in his eighties, and sat with his feet on a warm rug. The room was generally quite full, so that the schoolgirls who could not find seats on the benches on the women's side had to sit in the gallery at the back.

Rachel Rickman was rather feared by the children. She spoke in an old-fashioned chanting voice. In the days of Quietism Friends only spoke when under inspiration, and the style of delivery marked such ministry from ordinary speech. In the early days of the Society it was the custom for men to wear their hats in meeting, removing them only when vocal prayer was offered. We do not know at what time this practice ceased at Lewes, but we know that in the 1860's any Friend moved to minister would stand, and if they prayed they would kneel while the others stood.

There was little for the children, no Bible reading or singing, and the preaching was often beyond their understanding, but Maude Robinson remembered for the rest of her life how *a tall young man, with reddish hair, rose and spoke a few trembling sentences. This was Jonathan Hodgkin and his father, John Hodgkin, in the ministers gallery, broke into a beaming smile, as it was the first time that his son had ministered.*

The children, like the adults, went to meeting three times a week, on Wednesday and twice on Sunday. The meetings lasted only an hour; a century before they had lasted an hour and a half. Once home, meeting was not forgotten. Catherine Bastin (nèe Catherine Taylor) told of how they would play at Preparative Meeting, with a copy of the Book of Discipline. Her sister Mary was always the Clerk. She would call for the names of representatives to Monthly Meeting, and read the queries and replies in a voice of the utmost seriousness. Sometimes they played at 'just Meeting' and Mary would stand up and preach, imitating exactly the tones and gestures of John Hodgkin. He had a voice of singular strength and clearness; and under the pressure of religious feeling he generally exerted its full power. To some this seemed a waste of energy, but a deaf Friend commented, *we thank thee for speaking so loud. Thou art the only Minister in the Meeting whom we always hear.*

John Rickman died in 1859, and a few years later the ministers' gallery had, in order, Rachel Rickman, Mary Ann Speciall, Charlotte Smith, Matilda Rickman, and John Hodgkin, while Sarah Horne Rickman, Priscilla Godlee, Mary Trusted, Burwood Godlee, Richard Peters Rickman, and Charles Sturt sat in the front row. On the two side seats were Margaret and Joseph Woods. By 1870 Margaret Woods had died, Burwood Godlee had moved up to the back row, and Charles Sturt occupied the side seat.

This sketch of the Meeting has necessarily introduced many new names. We have a good deal of information about many of these people. It is now time to introduce the newcomers and add more detail to the portraits of those who have only been sketched so far.

An earlier chapter told of the boyhood of John and Thomas Hodgkin. John practised for many years as a lawyer in London. He was married at the age of 29 to Elizabeth Howard, but after 6 years she died, leaving him with 5 children. On her death-bed she had this special message for him, *just this: not to withhold anything, either public or private, which may be required for the good of our poor society.* Two years later he was recorded as a minister by Tottenham Meeting. He was married again, to Anne Backhouse, and in 1843 he became seriously ill. When he recovered he had the conviction that he had been spared to preach the Gospel, and with his wife's encouragement he retired to devote himself to this exclusively. Anne Hodgkin died in 1843, and he was married a third time, in 1850, to Elizabeth Haughton.

During the Irish famine of 1845-6 he assisted the relief committees in London and Dublin, and from 1846, perhaps earlier, he was an assistant clerk at Yearly Meeting. He spent some time in Galway, struggling hard, but in the end unsuccessfully, to teach improved methods of fishing. His legal friends tried to persuade him to return to the profession, and he was offered the post of judge in a court which had earlier been created on his recommendation, but he refused it. From 1850 to 1851 he served as Clerk of Yearly meeting, an unusually short term of office. He was succeeded by Joseph Thorp until 1862, when Edward Backhouse, a relative of his former wife, was appointed, while the Clerk to Meeting for Sufferings from 1862 to 1869 was Rickman Godlee, son of John Godlee.

In 1858 John Hodgkin returned to Lewes, living at first in Barcombe, and then renting Shelleys in the High Street at St Annes. This is a old house, with the date 1577 still visible over the door, which was once the home of Justice Henry Shelley. Alice Mary Hodgkin remembered it as a very happy home. It was a rambling old house, with a large paddock at the back, and beyond that a little farm, with cows, pigs and chickens, and a fruit and vegetable garden where the children played. The family lived a secluded life, and the children of the meeting only visited them occasionally to have tea in their hayfield, but one of the older visitors to the house was Alfred Waterhouse, a young architect who terraced some of the garden. He married John's daughter, Elizabeth, and eventually became Sir Alfred Waterhouse, now best known for the design of the Natural History Museum in London. Another of the elder daughters married Edward Fry, later Sir Edward Fry, the judge.

At the age of 61 John Hodgkin believed himself called to preach the gospel in America. This was a very difficult time for Friends in America, since, during the Civil War, their two great testimonies against war and against slavery tended to draw them in opposite directions. Though not a bad sailor, he had a peculiar aversion to travelling by sea; so much so that when he had once crossed the Atlantic he was often heard. to say that nothing but the fact that his wife and children were in England would have ever induced him to recross it.

During the last few years of his life he took an active part in the proceedings of the Social-Science Congress, until, in the summer of 1874 he had the *inexpressible grief* of losing Ellen, one of his younger daughters. He suffered a stroke and died in 1875.

Margaret and Joseph Woods, brother and sister, sat on the two single side seats. She is remembered as a pretty little old lady with blue eyes who, like most of the other women, always wore a black silk Quaker bonnet. They had a lady companion, Susan Mannington, large and motherly, who seemed to make them very comfortable.

Joseph Woods was born in 1776 at Stoke Newington. He was mainly self-taught, but became proficient in Latin, Greek, Hebrew, French, Italian, and modern Greek. He studied to be an architect, but having little business or technical ability he proved unsuccessful. He designed Clissold Park House for his uncle Jonathan Hoare, but in his design for the Commercial Salerooms in Mincing Lane he miscalculated the strength of some iron trestles and had to bear the cost of their replacement.

In 1806 he formed the London Architectural Society and he became its first president. He studied geology and botany in his spare time, and became the leading authority on British Roses. In 1833 he retired from architecture and settled at Lewes, devoting himself mainly to botany.

In 1850 he published the *Tourists' Flora*, a Descriptive Catalogue of the Flowering Plants and Ferns of the British islands, France, Germany, Switzerland, Italy, and the Italian Islands. He discovered several species of plant not previously noticed in Britain, and in his honour Robert Brown gave the name *Woodsia* to a rare and beautiful genus of British ferns.

When over 80 years of age he amused himself by finishing some of his early architectural sketches as presents to his friends and he was known as an exceptionally brilliant chess player. Joseph Woods died, unmarried, in 1864 in his house at 8 Priory Crescent, and is buried in front of the Meeting House.

After the death of Joseph Woods the side seat was occupied by Charles Sturt, the Postmaster of East Hoathly, who drove the nine or ten miles to Lewes in his pony cart each First Day. Catherine Taylor remembered him as a little old man, with long white hair and a gentle face, who came striding into Meeting. He had a broad-brimmed hat and a green coat which he wore over a neat grey suit.

Charles Sturt and his sister outside
East Hoathly Post Office

His duties as a postmaster and his salary were small, and he eked out a living by cultivating his bit of ground and selling the produce. He was a Convinced Friend (that is, he had become a Quaker by conversion, unlike most of the others, who were birthright members). He had little education, but he had read and pondered much on his Bible, on the writings of George Fox and of other early Friends. He used to keep up a running conversation on points of doctrine. For a while he was reluctant to speak in Meeting, except at Yearly Meeting time when the ministers were away. The children enjoyed his words, perhaps finding him easier to understand than they found the recorded ministers.

Sometimes he would come to dine with the Taylors, and *when his plate was handed to him he would spread his handkerchief over his knees, put his plate on it and start to eat. The children never laughed at him as they felt the influence of his sweet and quiet spirit. Sometimes he would send their mother a basket of fruit from his garden, and now and again he would write her a letter on a large old fashioned sheet of notepaper on the subject of the Christian bringing up of her children, which made her smile, but they all loved the old man.*

A much younger minister was Charlotte Smith, a widow who came to Lewes in order that her one child, Effie should attend school as a day-scholar. The children liked her sermons, remembering one on *What have they seen in thy house?*, using Hezekiah's mistake in display to the spies as a parable about the impression a truly Christian home should make on visitors. (To the confusion of everyone there were two Charlotte Smiths at the meeting, Charlotte Elizabeth Smith and Charlotte Josephine Smith, living together at a house called Green Bank in Rotten Row.)

In the ministers gallery were Sarah Rickman and Mary Ann Godlee, the sister of Burwood Godlee. They had retired from their school, and they had moved to the upper part of a house in Albion Street. Sarah Rickman was very clever with her hands. They had in their parlour a cardboard model of the Coliseum, which she had made, and at one time she had made a pair of high lace boots for a doll, turned out as beautifully as by any shoe maker. She was a great joy to the children with her varied interests; beautiful carving, and little figures and flowers she cut out of white paper for them with scissors, without drawing any outline, yet they were exquisite works of art.

Richard Peters Rickman, in the front row, was a rather forbidding looking old gentleman. Although in poor health he went to London Yearly Meeting in 1876. He was at both the preliminary sittings of Ministers and Elders, but the next day he became so ill that he was only just able to reach his house in Lewes. *After three hours, with a mind clear and peaceful, he breathed his last.* Obituaries of other Friends show that such occurrences were not uncommon.

Of his eight sisters Rachel, Sarah and Matilda outlived him. Their family home was Wellingham House which was bought by their father, John Rickman, in 1818. Visitors from Lewes sometimes came up the river, landing by a small wood which was a favourite picnic spot. The path from the wood led through the fields, past several summerhouses, to the house. One of these summerhouses survives (2010) just as they left it, and it can be seen in the summer by visiting the herb garden at Wellingham. Underneath is a grotto which the children decorated with shells and pieces of coloured glass. Outside is a flight of steps to the summerhouse which has four windows. The centre panes of glass are coloured. *If you looked through the blue, it seemed as if everything was covered with snow. The green turned the landscape into spring. The red glowed like summer, and the orange pane as if the harvest was just ready to be gathered in.* The house itself has hardly changed, but two rather disproportionate wings have been added on either side.

The summerhouse at Wellingham

Rachel Rickman had been born in Lewes, but was sent to school at York and Croydon. She returned home at the age of fourteen to help her mother with the large family, and moved to Wellingham with them when she was nineteen. She lived with her brother and a cousin for a while at Hastings, but returned home in 1835. For a while she and her sister Priscilla were concerned about bad housing at Ringmer. They had cottages built near the church to be let at low rents. In 1883 Rachel and Sarah provided a wheel pump (which still works) and pump house for the well on Ringmer Village Green *for the use of the inhabitants of Ringmer, and for wayfarers, for ever.*

Soon after her return home her sight began to fail, and in a few years she could read only embossed type, and she carried on her extensive correspondence by means of movable bars. She was called as a minister at an early age, but was not recorded as such until 1837. Later on Matilda also became blind, and after the death of their father and Priscilla they employed a young companion, Ellen Bellerby, to read aloud to them.

You would never have known from their actions or speech, that the sisters were blind. They always talked as if they saw clearly. Catherine Taylor was visiting there one evening with a number of friends, and as they sat at tea on their lawn, Rachel Rickman, one of the blind sisters said, "Now I want to show you something." So she led the way through their large kitchen garden to the edge of one of their fields where the wheat stood golden in the sunlight ready to be cut. Among the wheat grew hundreds of scarlet poppies. "Now", she said, "Isn't that a beautiful sight?".

John Rickman had two other daughters. Emily, who was the wife of Isaac Gray Bass, who with Marriage Wallis and Daniel Hack founded a high class wholesale and retail grocery under the name of Bass, Wallis and Hack in Market Street, Brighton. The other daughter, Benjamina, married Edward Lucas, of Luton, and became the grandmother of E.V. Lucas of literary fame.

Richard Peters Rickman of *The Friars* had a sister, Mary Hannah (1835-1905) who lived in *The Grey House*, which was demolished when Spences Field was built. (A boundary stone with the initials MHR is still visible on Malling Hill just outside 'Wayside'). Once a year on Twelfth Night she invited all of the children to her house for tea. Catherine Taylor recalled that:-

On the afternoon of the day, we were washed, brushed and dressed in our best and sent off with many admonitions as to behaviour, and told "not to eat too much cake." When we arrived, we sat down in the comfortable dining room to tea, our gracious hostess at the head of the table treating us just as if we had been grown up company, with her silent father at the other end. In one wall of the dining room had been made a large hole in which had been placed the stuffed head of a tiger, the opening in front being covered with glass and around the head had been placed imitation grasses and bulrushes, so that it looked as if the tiger was just coming out of his den. Mary Hannah Rickman told us she had bought it at an auction. She had wished to have the lion's head that was offered for sale at the same auction, but someone else had got that.

After tea where we had done full justice to all the good things including the Twelfth Night cake, the table was pushed on one side and we played some active games. One year I remember it was Brush. You stood the hearth brush in the middle of the floor and joined hands in a circle, and the fun lay in trying to make your neighbour knock it down and in keeping yourself from being pulled over it. Our hostess's silken skirts were long and voluminous, and I remember she took the coloured tablecloth off the table and pinned it tightly round herself, or else she would have no chance. After the romp we would go upstairs into the well lighted drawing room and play Lotto or Dominoes until about eight o'clock, when a supper of almonds and raisins, oranges, figs, etc., was brought up, after which she went with us into the bedroom and we put on our coats and bonnets. As we dressed alike she wondered how we would know our coats apart, and we told her that our mother had worked an initial into the waist lining. After this we went gaily home carrying with us the ornaments from the cake.

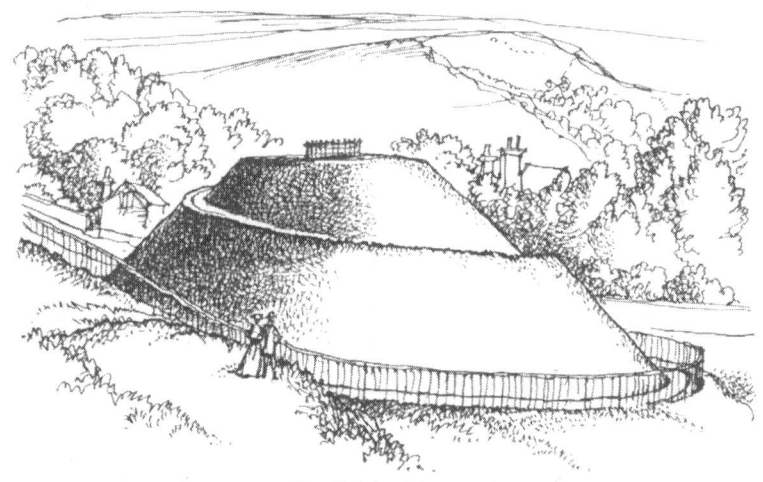

Charlie's burial mound
Drawing by C Walter Hodges

As an old lady one of her chief concerns was to rescue horses which had been ill-treated, or which were too old to work. They grazed in the fields surrounding the Grey House, and eventually, over the grave of her favourite horse, Charlie, she raised a large mound with a concrete centre and a winding path up to a seat at the top. It is strange that a Quaker horse should be so honoured when Quaker humans were commemorated only by small uniform grave-stones.

The Rickmans' House and the mound, part of a post card

When Sarah Rickman and Mary Ann Godlee gave up their school in The Friars it was taken over by Miriam, Mary and Josephine Dymond of Exeter, relatives of Jonathan Dymond whose *Essays on Christian Ethics* had for a time almost the authority of the Book of Discipline. Although the number of pupils appears never to have exceeded the twenties, the school's reputation was considerable. Benjamin and Candia Cadbury of Birmingham, for example, sent two of their daughters there. One of their pupils remembered the Dymonds as *capable and delightful women* and wrote that *few, if any, of their pupils can have left that school without having felt their gentle yet powerful influence, their loving and beautiful sympathy. They most surely brought away with them a recollection of many happy days spent in that beautiful country among the Sussex Downs, and of walks and glad converse with their girl friends.*

Eventually the Dymonds returned to Exeter, and their place was taken by Rachel Speciall. In 1855 she was joined by Mary and Catherine Trusted. (A pupil noted the Dickensian appropriateness of their names, but refrained from commenting on that of their friend, the Reverend Arthur Perfect!)

A prospectus for the school survives, and it reads as follows:-
  Boarding School for the Daughters of Friends
  Lewes, Sussex
  Conducted by Mary & Catherine Trusted & Rachel Speciall
  The design of this institution is to supply a good Education on moderate Terms for the Daughters of Friends and those professing with them in conformity with the principles of the Society. It is the desire of those concerned

in it, that religious improvement shall be prominently kept in view, and simplicity of dress and manners encouraged.

Terms
For Board and English Education £35.0.0   per Annum
Washing   2.0.0   " "
Drawing   4.0.0   " "
The Latin Language   3.0.0   " "
French & German each   4.0.0   " "

The French and German Languages are taught by Natives of the respective Countries, and Drawing by an efficient Master. English books are provided at the expense of the Proprietors. A vacation of Six Weeks in Summer, and Three Weeks in Winter, but pupils may remain at the School during the latter if preferred. Three months' notice, or payment for that time, is expected previous to removal of a pupil.

Application for the admission of children may be made to the Superintendent, or to Daniel Pryor Hack, Brighton, Isaac Gray Bass, do, Burwood Godlee, Lewes, to whom all remittances may be made direct, or they may be paid at the London & County Bank, 21 Lombard Street, to the credit of Friends' School, Lewes.

Rachel Speciall was joined by her sister Mary Ann who had been educated at E. and A. Rickman's school at Rochester, and had taught at the Friends' school at Ackworth.

Catherine Trusted was born in 1824. She had much difficulty in mastering spelling and the multiplication table. After a care-free childhood she became very determined to overcome any obstacles. She abandoned reading fiction since the stories interfered with her thoughts in meeting, and she was observed later in life with a Latin Grammar to hand as she did the housework. *Considering time as one of the most important talents entrusted to their care, she thought much of punctuality, and would encourage her pupils when leaving school for the greater freedom of home, to make for themselves a plan for each day, and yet always keep themselves ready to fall in with those of others when it seemed best. Accounts kept under her care were spoken of as "a curiosity for exactness;" it was her practice to write a letter for every one received.* Her first job was as a governess, and for a while she worked in Emilie Schnell's school in Brighton before moving to Ackworth where she *enjoyed the refined and intellectual companionship of Mary Ann Speciall.*

Maude Robinson, a local author very popular earlier this century, wrote:-

Never did parents specially entrust their children to more utterly conscientious and kindly teachers than those three Quaker ladies, dressed in the primmest, neatest gowns, who always addressed their pupils as "thee" and "thou."

The house, now the Lewes post-office, was not ideal for a school, but was much larger than it looks from the street. Still, twenty-five boarders were a tight fit, and there were desks for only half a dozen day scholars, bearing the well-known Lewes names of Macrae, Crosskey, Kidd and Hillman. A younger sister of our Miss Speciall, Miss Caroline, kept a separate school in The Crescent, with a few boarders and many day scholars. A few of her elder pupils used to come to share our more advanced lessons with masters and lecturers, and once a week we went for a country walk together.

A Quaker school in the High Street – now the post office.
Drawing by C Walter Hodges

It was in August, 1872, that I stood at the corner of Watergate Lane, watching the carriage drive away in which my parents had brought the last of their eight children to start on a boarding school career. My hair had been cropped for the first time to the conventional length for school-girls, just touching my shoulders, and the two front locks were tied back with a coloured ribbon. What a quaint little figure I should look to modern eyes! A Dolly Varden hat, a blue cambric polonaise, edged with a frill, and bunched up in many folds behind the waist, worn over a striped skirt, white stockings and elastic-sided boots!

I was the only boarder from Sussex; the group we met came from Darlington, Birmingham, at least a dozen from Essex and several nice Irish girls who came 'to get the brogue rubbed off' they said. Some of the older girls who remembered my sister were kind in telling me who was who, and in initiating me into the school routine and what we might and might not do. We had no system of prefects, but a good deal of responsibility rested on the girls who had, some of them, turned up their hair and wore the hideous 'chignon' fashionable in the seventies.

In the large play-room we had a strong oaken plank on which two sets of three or four girls jumped against each other, with much noise and laughter; and a perfectly ideal swing on which we played many dangerous pranks, but I never remember anyone coming to grief.

The day after my school entry I was set down to an entrance examination with other new girls. Here, like many home-taught children, my attainment was very uneven. In some studies, geography, German and drawing I was well before the rest, but woefully behind in the ordinary grounding of those girls who had been in a preparatory school, and this was a handicap all through my school career. It was Miss Rachel Speciall, a very clever woman, who mostly taught the two upper classes. She was frail and suffering, but an enthusiast, and enjoyed teaching the clever and advanced girls. She schooled herself to be very patient with the naturally stupid ones, but to those of middling abilities her sharp tongue was a terror - she could never believe that we were doing our best. Still, she could be very kind, and unselfishly gave up an hour of her Sunday afternoons to those children who voluntarily went to her parlour to read the German Bible, and learn German hymns.

Miss Mary Trusted was the housekeeper, and an excellent one. Our food, if plain, was always good and well cooked, and she looked after our health, if in what would now be considered a very old-fashioned way. Her own handwriting was exquisite, and she tried hard to make ours the same - a good running hand, yet every letter distinct. She also taught us needlework - of which we had a good deal, and if we have ever scamped neat stocking mending and perfect button-holes it is not Miss Mary's fault.

Miss Catherine was the humblest and most unselfish of good women, teaching the younger classes with a thoroughness which irritated some girls, but who, among them, does not remember the geography she taught? She also taught us grammar - real old-fashioned Lindley Murray, and Butter's Spelling with the very interesting derivations of the words. Miss Catherine taught me another useful lesson - to laugh at small misfortunes. I had carelessly smashed a handsome vase, and expected a well-deserved scolding. When she saw my woebegone face the kind woman burst out

91

laughing: 'That is the way to meet small misfortunes,' she said, with never a word of reproof, but far more effectual.

Lewes was near enough to Brighton to have regular visits from good masters. I remember with pleasure a set of mildly scientific experiments on light, heat and electricity. Every week a drilling-master came, and in the great playroom, without any music, or apparatus, he taught us to walk, and avoid the ungainly tricks of fast growing girls. The drilling-master had a wife, who, as we did not learn dancing, gave us an occasional lesson in "Deportment," making bows and curtseys, edging sideways between crooked seats (a very useful lesson that), handing a book gracefully, and even walking up and down stairs.

A French master came weekly, and our translations, compositions and French poetry were scrupulously prepared for him, but in my day we did not like him, and accused him of giving good marks to the pretty girls. He even stroked a flowing lock of wavy hair, to the owner's deep disgust. it was far otherwise with the drawing-master, quiet Mr Fisher. I think he was Head of Brighton School of Art in those days.

A girls school without outside examinations, or a single piano! How strange that must seem to many, but only about a third of the pupils learned music, and lessons and practice went on at the house of the music teacher opposite.

Almost all the boarders were of Quaker families and it was a matter of course to go twice on Sundays and on Wednesdays to the Friends Meeting in Friars Walk, and I for one am grateful for the influence of the quiet hours spent there. The three had contrived that each of the elder girls should have a quarter of an hour in the evening alone in her bedroom - "Meditations" we called it, and some of the more volatile did not care for it, to others it became a deep privilege.

The school regime was rather Spartan. At 7 a.m. summer and winter we were expected to be in the schoolroom. Miss Catherine was always there before us, at her desk, fixing needlework for the little pupils of the British School. We stood for a few minutes, and repeated together a psalm, or very often the whole of the long morning hymn from "The Christian Year," for the ideal of sanctifying 'the trivial round, the common task" was one of the ideals our teachers wished to instil. An hour of strenuous "prep" as it would now be called, followed, and we were quite ready for the breakfast consisting only of what we called "doorsteps" - large slices of excellent bread and butter, with cups of mild tea or coffee.

On Mondays and Tuesdays we spoke only French, of not very good quality, I fear, and on Fridays German, which did not trouble me as I had had a German governess at home.

It was a very different Lewes in the seventies. Tar-barrels were rolled down the street in the most irresponsible way, and a big bonfire lit before the Town Hall on

November the fifth. In that open space and along the street the Cattle Market was held, leaving it sadly unclean.

In 1874 there was a severe outbreak of fever in Lewes and the school was removed to Brighton, where, rather more than two years later, Rachel Speciall died, and it was closed. During the busy days of school-keeping the sisters had been careful to keep up their interest in outside work. Mary Trusted much enjoyed her position as Secretary to a small Girls Home at Delap Hall in South Street, named after Dr. Delap, a John Aubrey-like character who lived there until 1812. Mary Trusted also showed a warm interest in the Bible Society. She took her share in the Meetings for Discipline in her district, and until within a few years of her death she was Secretary to the Lewes branch of the Missionary Helpers Union. She was diligent in sewing and knitting for others, and, although rather short-sighted she made her own Quaker caps until within a few months of her death. Among the many other interests which engaged Catherine Trusted after her return to Lewes was a small Band of Hope at the workhouse, in which she taught the boys the advantages of total abstinence, especially from its physiological side.

During the 1870's there was a strong evangelical movement within the society, and Maude Robinson recalls:-

I think, during my second autumn at school there was something of a revival in the meeting, and a great desire that we young things should share in the faith that was so lovingly preached to us. But it was not the words of local Friends that brought Life's great message to me. One Wednesday morning, a Friend visiting meetings was present, perhaps one of the "Not mighty or noble," but as he spoke I saw for the first time that I was called to bring my sins to the foot of the Cross and devote my life to the best of Masters. I went through my lessons with the French master that afternoon like one in a dream, and in the solitary time of "meditations", as I knelt by the window looking out over the hills, which I used to so much enjoy, I definitely devoted my life to the service of the Lord Jesus Christ, and in spite of many failures and unfaithfulness I have never drawn back.

Years after, when the Angel of Death had for the first time entered our two homes on the same day, and sorrow had drawn us together, I found that to another girl that meeting had been the great turning point, and our friendship to this day is a very close one. We neither felt we could speak to any one of the great change - I think we were afraid of making a profession, and not living up to it. But I think since then, I have never entered Lewes Meeting House without the thought "Thanks be unto God for His unspeakable Gift."

Now that I am an old woman, and look back over sixty years to that day I feel it is right to tell this story, and to express a hope that deeper spiritual life may come to all who attend Lewes Meeting, and that to many in your Meeting Room may come the faithfully delivered messages which made it the scene of the great turning point of my own life.

Second in the ministers gallery sat Caleb Rickman Kemp, who had been born in 1836. His father, Grover Kemp, was John Glaisyer's partner at Brighton. Caleb Kemp, after two year's work in a drapers shop, moved to Mitcham where he learned the craft of flour-milling. He attended Croydon Meeting where he was strongly influenced by Peter Bedford. At the age of 17, unusually young, he began to speak in Meeting. *I should not think,* he wrote in his journal, *that anyone ever entered upon the work of the ministry with a deeper feeling of poverty, or with less acquaintance with the truths contained in the Holy Bible, than myself; often do I feel as if a discouraging word would upset me altogether.* He was recorded a Minister at the age of 21, an almost exceptional occurrence. Jonathan Hodgkin wrote: *There are those among us who can remember looking upon Caleb Kemp with wonder as the only member of the Society who was recorded a Minister at an early age.*

Later that year he joined his father in a religious visit to the West Indies. They visited many of the islands, holding meetings with both white and coloured people in Antigua, Montserrat, Nevis, St Kitts, Barbados, Granada and Trinidad, thus beginning his life-long interest in the welfare of the coloured population of the West Indies and his connection with the Anti-Slavery Society, on whose committee he served for twenty-seven years.

When he returned he was invited to join his cousins in the old established lime-burning, corn and coal business of Rickman and Company at Lewes, taking the place previously held in the firm by his cousin Richard Rickman. While he was considering this he attended a week day meeting of which he wrote *our friend John Hodgkin is away from Lewes and I had to sit first in the gallery; a position I had rarely occupied; and one that brings a feeling of weight over my mind not easy to describe – I was the youngest at meeting on my side.*

He became a partner in the company, together with John Clay Lucas and George Newington. Newington was not a Friend, although his wife and children were members of the Meeting. Caleb Kemp records in his journal that Richard Rickman owned a house at the bottom of the High Street. it was occupied by Doctor Macrae, but the lease was coming to an end. Rickman offered the house to his friend, and Caleb Kemp accepted, but later, considering that removal would be a hardship to Macrae, asked to be released from his agreement. In the following spring he was married to Jane Morland of Croydon. Her family originated the Morland sheepskin business, and is intermarried with the Clarks, also Quakers, whose shoe business still thrives.

For nearly half a century Caleb and Jane Kemp lived at Lewes, the greater part of the time, since 1865, in a house in Rotten Row, designed for them by William Beck and called Bedford Lodge in honour of Peter Bedford who had died in the previous year. It was not long after the removal to Bedford Lodge that Grover Kemp also passed away. Caleb Kemp wrote in his journal: *I do not believe that a single colourable act can be pointed to, in the whole of my father's life, or that he made a single enemy.*

One of his friends wrote *The home of Lewes became a centre of much genial hospitality. He was an excellent story-teller, and possessed a great store of racy anecdotes with which to entertain his many guests.'* [The word 'Racy' at that date did not have the later connotation of 'slightly indecent'.] *Maude Robinson remembered, 'How kind he was to the shy schoolgirls, who went in groups to tea at his house, in playing games with US. I remember once in "Clumps" he chose to be questioned on the fish weathercock on Southover Church, and it was so much larger than we had imagined that we were completely puzzled.*

Those who knew him only in meeting might have found those statements strange: in his religion he was utterly serious, but in other situations his tolerance and his sense of humour made him very popular. No one, with the possible exception of his wife, saw his journal, but it now reveals a mischievous sense of humour on subjects which, publicly, even he had to treat seriously.

Like many others in the meeting he was concerned with temperance, and this subject throws some light on the strange contrast between legalistic rigidity and complete personal freedom which still exists in the Society today. Testimonies held from the beginning were extraordinarily difficult to change, even if the circumstances had altered to the point where they threatened the life of the Society. In 1874 Yearly Meeting warned Friends of the evils of drink, but, while it noted regretfully that some Friends were still working in the trade, it would not instruct them to leave it.

On the other hand there was still an absolute prohibition on music, rigidly adhered to by the older Friends, but quietly ignored by the younger ones. When the YMCA began in Lewes it used the Meeting

House. Its first secretary was Joseph Hopkins, a farmer who retired in 1875 to devote himself to this work. He was soon recorded a minister, and became clerk of the preparative meeting. In 1883 Richard Peters Rickman mentioned that the YMCA had dared to use a harmonium on premises belonging to Friends and the Meeting required Joseph Hopkins to tell his own committee that the practice should not be repeated. Technically Richard Peters Rickman was right, but attempts of this kind to uphold the old testimonies did great harm to the Society. He was not alone in this: Burwood Godlee who was Vice-Chairman and Treasurer of the Lewes Dispensary was conspicuously absent from a charity concert in its aid, as late as 1881.

Many Friends belonged to the Movement for the Ban of the Sale of Intoxicating Liquor on Sunday, the Lewes Total Abstinence Society, the British Women's Temperance Association and the Blue Ribbon Society. Many upheld the new testimony to the value of temperance in more sympathetic ways. The Coach House in the Meeting grounds was built to stable horses which, in former times, would have been left at public houses.

Eliza Payne, with her own money, paid for the building of the British Workman's Institute in Little East Street, *A public house without intoxicants open daily from six to ten. Coffee, refreshments and entertaining games. Good Templar's Lodges are held here. The building is the property of Miss Payne and was built by that lady to encourage temperance.* The building was later a Baptist chapel, and is now converted into flats.

When a Coffee Tavern was opened in the town, Burwood Godlee contributed a hundred weight of coffee and Caleb Kemp gave a hundred weight of coal. Caleb Kemp, with other friends, took part in many activities which brought them into social contact with outsiders, activities which would have been forbidden to the stricter Friends a few years before. They attended the Mechanics Institute, the Workman's Institute, the Chess Club, poetry evenings, the Sussex Archaeological Society, and the Monday Evening Club - a discussion group which numbered amongst its members only those with considerable wealth or status.

The Coffee Tavern
Drawing by C Walter Hodges

One substantial new departure was their involvement in local politics. In 1881 the Borough of Lewes received its Incorporation Act. Caleb Kemp was the only Quaker to stand for election. His election address reads:

Ladies and Gentlemen,
It was my intention to have taken no part in the present municipal contest - except that of casting my vote, but having, with others, received a requisition influentially signed by nearly 300 ratepayers, asking me to become a candidate for the Council, I have decided, upon further consideration, to place my services at the disposal of the ratepayers, and I now solicit their confidence and support.
In doing so I am not insensible to the prior claims of those gentlemen - of whom some are now before the constituency as candidates - who have heretofore held office.
I am, ladies and gentlemen,
Yours very respectfully,
Caleb R. Kemp

He was immediately made an alderman, and two years later was elected Mayor, in spite of the Conservative majority on the Council and his openly Liberal politics.

He wrote in his journal:-

I went to the inaugural dinner, but such things are not in my line. And how I should manage to be Mayor I don't see. Sufficient for the day is the evil thereof. At the meeting of the Council I took some part, and felt at home in the work. Many considerations present themselves: one is that we should not make our scruples or our religious tastes too prominent, so as to attract notice to ourselves. Another is that we should take things that come to us, simply. In both of these I have much to learn.

I was unanimously elected with very nice feeling on the part of my colleagues. At the dinner all went nicely. My having taken out 'Army and Navy' [from the toast] *and put in 'Literature, Science and Art' was pleasantly alluded to.*

Caleb Rickman Kemp
Photograph by Reeves of Lewes

On First Day I drove to Brighton, and preached at some length in their morning meeting. I brought Marriage Wallis back with me, and at three o'clock we attended at our Meeting-house and met the Corporation in order publicly to acknowledge our dependence upon Almighty God, and unitedly to seek His blessing on our Municipal year. We walked in procession from the Town Hall. The place was crowded. I offered prayer in reference to the Council, its work, and the town generally. J. G. Hopkins read very well the twelfth and thirteenth of Romans; and M. Wallis spoke well and practically from 'Diligent in business, fervent in spirit, serving the Lord.' He then offered prayer. I feeling humbled and thankful, and others I know, and as far as I know, all satisfied.

As a magistrate his help was much valued. After Burwood Godlee he was the only teetotaller, the only nonconformist, and the only man engaged in *what is technically called trade* on the Lewes bench.

He understood the more conventional worship of the other churches, as an incident from 1883 relating to the Tabernacle indicates. *The Congregational Minister here was taken ill on Seventh day night - not alarmingly, but so as to cause his leaving the house and preaching on First day quite out of the question. His wife - a friend of ours - called on me on First day morning to explain matters; to ask if I could supply her husband's place. She put it - whether the circumstances did not indicate that the Lord had a service for me. They had no one among their own people, to whom they could look - and there was no time to communicate with places at a distance. - I accepted the position - and, after an interview with the deacons, met the very interesting, large, and as it proved, very enthusiastic congregation.*

THE TABERNACLE.

In 1888 he became Clerk of the Meeting for Sufferings, an office which he held for five years. His retirement from business in 1889 gave him more leisure for such engagements; and for many years his journeys to London and back were very frequent. In 1890 he became Clerk of London Yearly Meeting, a post which he filled with power and dignity for nine years. He had been an assistant clerk for the previous eighteen years. His own statement on retiring from the Clerkship in 1899 is an illustration of the thoroughness with which he did anything he undertook: he said that since he first took his seat at the Clerk's table he had been absent only three times, and then only during his Assistant Clerkship, during his twenty-seven years of office. He was succeeded by John Morland, a relative of his wife.

Clear and decided in his judgment, he readily gathered the sense of the Meeting, and embodied it in a minute, with rapidity and with facility of expression. His careful thought of Yearly Meeting minutes did not end with the draft. As is well known, the minutes are, at the conclusion of each sitting, subjected to the scrutiny of a revision committee. But minutes requiring special care in wording often received close personal consideration in the evening, each word being carefully weighed, until, whilst maintaining intact the sense of the draft minute, the polished form which it finally assumed, satisfied its critical author. it was noteworthy how he brought the

Yearly Meeting back to normal conditions when some ripple of excitement had passed over that dignified assembly. On one occasion when an address of considerable interest had been delivered, somewhat in the style of a popular orator, and the atmosphere of the Yearly Meeting seemed to have lost its wonted calm, he asked for a few moments of silence, after which he knelt in prayer. Solemnity was restored.

One of his main interests was the British and Foreign Bible Society, which Friends had actively supported since its foundation in 1804. He had joined the committee in 1880, and in 1892 he became the chairman. It was not merely his love and reverence for the Bible which made this work dear to him, but also the fact that it brought together Christians who in other respects were separated by sectarian differences. Eventually he was made a Vice-President of the Society, and his portrait was hung on the wall of the committee room.

His activities with other denominations were not welcomed by all. In his earlier years more traditional Friends felt that recognising other denominations was a denial of their belief that the Quaker way was the only true one, and they feared any evangelical fervour.

His obituary in The Times states: *The Bible Society's committee is composed entirely of laymen, of whom half are members of the Church of England and half represent the various denominations and the foreign Christians resident in London. Over a company of these diverse opinions a Quaker is apt to be found an ideal moderator, and Mr Kemp had had large experience in a similar capacity elsewhere. To great dignity of manner and quiet sincerity of belief he added considerable business capacity. It fell to him from time to time to receive on behalf of the committee distinguished visitors, returning officials, and newly-appointed workers. At most times it would have been hard to know what denomination he represented, but now and again the Quaker in him would appear when, instead of calling upon some member to commend a new worker in prayer, he would ask him if he felt "moved" to do so.*

He was for some years the chairman and treasurer of the Lewes Town Mission, and in 1897 he helped to set up the Lewes Evangelical Free Church Council. In the same year he played an important part in making the Lewes Subscription Library into a free library for the whole town. The Library had existed since 1795, but it was in financial difficulties. The Public Libraries Act empowered the council to take it over, but not to pay the outstanding costs, estimated then as £200 to £300. Caleb Kemp agreed to pay off the debts and to put the building (Fitzroy House) into good repair, at a cost which he later noted to be £450, and the town accepted the library as part of the celebrations for

Queen Victoria's Jubilee. A red granite tablet was unveiled to commemorate this, but Caleb Kemp was not there to see it.

He had received an invitation from the Bishop of London to be on the steps of St Paul's Cathedral at the thanksgiving service. The Mayor was pleased to think that an inhabitant of their own town and a member of the Corporation had been allotted such an important seat to witness this memorable pageant. Caleb Kemp notes with amusement in his journal *that there were only 30 non-conformists present, and that the Anglicans had the lion's share of the places.*

Later, with the Archbishop of Canterbury and Lord Northampton he was one of a deputation which presented a Bible to King Edward in the year of his coronation.

In 1905 he wrote, *How near I have missed being Sir Caleb I do not know - But it has just come to my knowledge that a year ago Lord Northampton did his 'best' to induce the Prime Minister to recommend me for a knighthood in connection with the centenary of the B & F B Society – Lord Northampton says that he at one time thought he had succeeded – "but I failed" - of course the Prime Minister was a Tory – and Lord Northampton & this humble friend (myself) are firmly Liberal - whether or not that influenced the Prime Minister I do not know.*

At this time he was chairman of the board of magistrates, and on November the 5th several rowdies were arrested. When Caleb Kemp heard the charges he had to advise the court that legally there was no case to answer. As a long-standing opponent of the celebrations it was greatly to his embarrassment when the crowds waiting outside for the verdict cheered him as a *Friend of Bonfire*.

By this time he was a comparatively rich man. In 1899 his income was £2000 and his expenditure £1500, and he was determined to give more away. He wrote in 1907 that *I do not wish my property to be above or slightly in excess of £50,000 & it is now 'within sight' of that amount.* When he died in October 1908 the gross value of his estate on his death was £48,510, of which he left £2,000 to the British and Foreign Bible Society, £1,000 each to the Friends Foreign Mission Association and the London City Mission, £500 each to the Friends Home Missionary Society and the Society of Friends Yearly Meeting, and many smaller bequests. A clock which he presented to the town can still be seen in the Council Chamber at the Town Hall.

The Twentieth Century

Lewes Meeting House as it is today.

Over a period of 40 years the Friends of wealth and importance in the town and in the Society had died, leaving Lewes Meeting only a shadow of its former self. In spite of the many good qualities of its members it had failed to rear a generation of successors. Perhaps it was the glowing memories of the older Friends which led them to despair of the future. In 1918 a meeting was held at Bedford Lodge to decide whether it should be closed. Numerically it was little smaller than in the time of its former greatness, but it briefly ceased to exist as a preparative meeting - one which had its own clerk and held its own business meeting. Fortunately they decided to continue the Meeting and it eventually flourished again.

During the Great War many Quakers, because of their religion, were accepted as conscientious objectors, but some were not accepted and others refused to register. Friends spent much time assisting objectors both in prison and in work camps. One of these was Edward Glaisyer who had moved to Lewes at the age of 69 at the request of local Friends. For a while he was 'Quaker Chaplain' at the prison, and he also befriended the young men at the Home office work centre at Denton, to which many conscientious objectors were drafted, and where at least one died because of harsh conditions and inadequate medical attention. Towards the end of the war, Friends published leaflets in defiance of the censorship regulations, and as a result, during part of the 1918 Yearly Meeting the Clerk was not at the table, but at the Old Bailey. Thus Mary Jane Godlee, a descendent of John Godlee, became the first woman to preside over Yearly Meeting.

Since then the meeting has grown, and in recent years the number of members has been over 70, and there have been many attenders. Several changes in the building have been necessary to provide better facilities, but great care has been taken to ensure that the new is harmoniously integrated with the old. In Victorian times the interior panelling, the furniture and the exterior mathematical tiling had been painted. The first real restoration began during the last war. The fire-watchers stationed at the Meeting House spent many nights scraping away brown paint to reveal the wood beneath. After the war the paint was removed from the mathematical tiling, and the porch, once black, was repainted in white.

The burial ground, which was difficult to maintain, was reshaped. Most of the space in front of the Meeting House has been used for burials, but the earlier graves were never marked by headstones, since Friends, for many years, had a testimony against their use. A carefully measured plan was kept, showing the location of each grave.

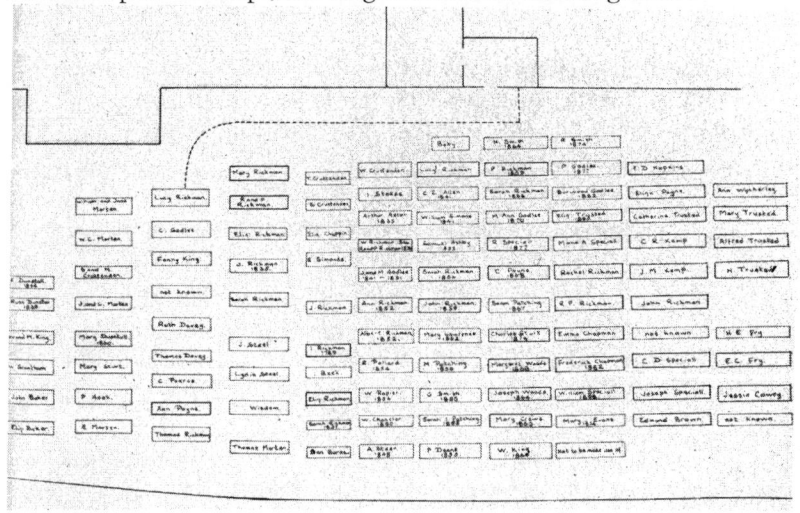

When stones were eventually permitted the regulations specified that the design should be uniform in each burial ground, and that the inscriptions should be limited to name, age, and date of death. Nevertheless, one of the stones, in memory of Jessie Cowey who died in 1929, also bears the inscription *Resurgam*, a daring innovation which must have provoked some controversy at the time. In 1956 the scattered stones were removed from the centre of the lawn, and placed neatly in rows in front of the wall. As the remains beneath were not disturbed no Home office license was needed for this work, but permission was sought from all surviving relatives.

The Coach House was a more difficult problem. For many years after the last horse had been stabled there it was used, as the only sizeable alternative to the meeting room, for Sunday School classes and other purposes. For many years there was discussion about an internal conversion which would preserve the outward appearance, and about the provision of badly needed car parking spaces. Cost was originally the reason for delay, but eventually the idea had to be abandoned when structural weaknesses were found. The building was demolished, but two unusual window frames were preserved, in the hope that eventually they may be incorporated in another building. This allowed the sale of land to the Council for an access road to the ground at the back of the Meeting House, and for the provision of car parking spaces.

The Coach House, shortly before its demolition

The end wall of the Warden's cottage was removed, and the building was lengthened. At the front of the meeting room a door was made through to the new extension. For the first time there was an adequate kitchen, a library/committee room, and a large hall provided primarily for the Sunday School, but also used by many others. On the first floor, instead of the small rooms of the original cottage, there is now a spacious flat for the Wardens.

For more than a century the Meeting House has been let to other organisations. Many of these have no connection with Friends, but others are very close to Quaker concerns. Whenever Friends have been aware of social needs which are not being met they have offered the premises at concessionary rates or without charge. In the past many Quaker groups were founded to deal with social problems, but this approach is no longer favoured: Friends prefer to join existing groups, or to found groups which are far less exclusive.

The interior of the Meeting Room at present.

Friends have been known for their peace testimonies since the seventeenth century, but in recent years many new peace groups have been founded in Lewes. There are few which are without Quakers, and few in which Quakers have not taken important initiatives, but there are none locally which are exclusive to Friends.

How much remains of the vision of the first Quakers? The distinctive dress and speech are gone, as is the abrasive anti-clericalism. Art and music are now encouraged rather than forbidden. The old exclusiveness has been replaced by a warmer universalism, with respect to doctrine as well as to society in general. Nevertheless, most Friends would argue that the essentials have been preserved, and that the changes have been made only to allow better expression of the fundamentals.

Meeting for Worship is held in much the same way as before. Meetings are silent, except when a person feels spontaneously moved to rise and speak. Quaking is not a phenomenon of the seventeenth century alone. Business meetings still follow the same organisation, and the methods which were used to seek out agreement rather than confrontation still work, although no method is a sure guarantee against human frailty.

The Clerk and Assistant Clerk at the table

The concerns of the first Friends are still keenly felt: respect for the individual, especially regarding freedom of worship and belief. The most repeated of the sayings of George Fox is, *"Walk cheerfully over the world, seeking that of God in every one."* From that comes the concern for social justice which embraces all, which will not accept the domination of one class, group, or nation by others, and which makes it impossible for most Friends to take up arms. No creed or other formal statement of belief has ever been accepted by Friends. The discovery by George Fox that God was to be found, not in books, churches, or through priests, but within, has been the source of individual Quaker faith and practice. At first its expression was in conventional Christian terms, but worshippers at Lewes each Sunday now include conventional Christians, those who would express their beliefs in other terms, members of other faiths, and those who are unsure about any belief but who nevertheless find that meeting answers their needs. The important question for Quakers is not whether they have the same beliefs, but only whether they can work and worship together. Future generations in Lewes may inhabit a world as strange to us as ours would be to George Fox, but it is unlikely that the principles which brought the Seekers into the Society of Friends will have been superseded.

Bibliography

Colin Brent, Lewes dissenters outside the law, 1663-86, Sussex Archaeological Collections **123** (1985), 195-214

W. K. Rector, Lewes Quakers in the seventeenth and eighteenth centuries, Sussex Archaeological Collections **116** (1978), 195-214, 31-40

East Sussex Record Office, Records of the Society of Friends

W. C. Braithewaite, The Beginnings of Quakerism to 1660, William Sessions, 1981.

W. C. Braithewaite, The Second Period of Quakerism, William Sessions, 1979.

Michael Rose, Curator of the Dead: Thomas Hodgkin (1798-1866). Peter Owen, 1981.

Dictionary of National Biography

The Annual Monitor

Walter Salter, Lewes Meeting, 1934.

A

Abbott, Benjamin, 73, 74
Act of Uniformity, 12
Adams, John, 20
Agates, Henry, 35, 36, 37
Akehurst, Alexander, 41
Akehurst, Mary, 18, 19, 20, 28, 29, 32, 41, 43, 44
Akehurst, Ralph, 18, 19, 37, 38, 39, 41
Akehurst, Thomas, 35, 36, 37, 38, 39, 40, 41, 43
Albion Street, 45, 73, 79, 84
Alexander I, 69
All Saints, 21, 22, 23, 29, 35, 38, 39, 40, 43, 79
Allen, William, 71
American Indians, 71
American War of Independence, 66
Anne of Cleves' House, 73
Anti-Slavery Society, 94
Archbishop of Canterbury, 101
Ashfold, William, 14
Astie, Sam, 38
Astie, Samuel, 31, 32, 35, 37, 38, 39, 40, 41, 42
Aston, Eliza, 74
Avery, Thomas, 23

B

Backhouse, Anne, 81
Backhouse, Edward, 81
Band of Hope, 93
Baptists, 12
Barcomb, 55
Barcombe, 27, 56, 57, 62, 81
Barratt, Thomas, 31
Bass, Isaac Gray, 86, 89
Bass, Wallis and Hack, 86
Bastin, Catherine, 80
Bax, Richard, 14
Bear Inn, 49
Bear Yard, 66
Beard, Nicholas, 23, 28, 31, 41, 43

Beard, Thomas, 41, 43
Bedford Lodge, 95, 103
Bedford, Peter, 94, 95
Bellerby, Ellen, 73, 86
Bermondsey, 73
Bible Society, 93, 100
Birmingham, 88, 91
Bish, Henry, 42
Bishop of London, 100
Blatchington, 25
Blue Ribbon Society, 96
Bonwick, Richard, 14
Boughton, Richard, 19
Boxall, Thomas, 62
Braithwaite, William, 47
Bridge Hotel, 76
Bridger, James, 45, 46
Bridger, Richard, 21, 38, 39, 40
Brighthelmstone, 54, 55, 56
Brighton, 58, 67, 68, 69, 71, 75, 86, 89, 92, 93, 94, 98
Brightridg, Thomas, 20
British and Foreign Bible Society, 100, 101
British School in Lancaster Street, 77
British Workmans Institute, 96
Brown, Robert, 83
Browne, Richard, 44
Bryant, Ferdinando, 28
Bryant, William, 21
Budd, Thomas, 29
Burns, Ann, 54, 55, 56
Burns, Daniel, 50, 57, 59, 62

C

Cadbury, Benjamin, 88
Calvinists, 57
Capel, 14
Carleton, Bishop Guy, 23
Carleton, Justice, 44
Castle Green, 18
Castle Place, 73
Catholic Apostolic Church, 54
Chess, 97
Chichester, 11, 33, 55

Clark, James, 23, 28, 29, 31, 33
Cliffe Bridge, 11, 49, 72
Cliffe, The, 19
Coach House, 105
Coates, Jane, 56, 67
Coffee Tavern, 97
Collgeat, Robert, 45, 46
Cook, Captain James, 66
Cooper, Susanah, 20
Coppard, John, 33
Cottingham, Ann, 20
Coulstock, Mary, 19
Cowey, Jessie, 105
Croft, The, 15
Crosskey, 90
Croydon Meeting, 94
Cruttenden, Susanna, 55, 56
Cruttenden, Thomas, 61, 62
Cuckfield, 23, 35, 38

D

Dapson, Mary, 19
Darnell, Councillor, 42
Delap Hall, 93
Delves, John, 28
Dial House, 72, 73
Diggers, 12
Ditchling, 31
Dobell, Captain Walter, 46
Dover, 69, 70
Dragoons, 59
Duchess of Oldenburg, 69
Dymond, Jonathan, 88
Dymond, Mary, 88
Dymond, Miriam, 88

E

E. and A. Rickman's school, 89
Eager, Jane, 41
Eager, Stephen, 14, 20, 21
East Hoathly, 79, 83
Edward VI, 11
Edward VII, 101
Elizabeth, Queen, 11, 41, 44
Ellis, Elias, 28
Ellis, John, 23, 29, 32, 41
Emperor of Russia, 69

Episcopalians, 11
Eresby, John, 35, 36, 37, 40, 42, 43, 44
Essays on Christian Ethics, 88
Etheringtonians, 12

F

Faraday, Michael, 73, 74
Farley, John, 36, 37
Fifth Monarchists, 12
Fisher, Mr (Art Teacher), 92
Fitzroy House, 75, 100
Fletching, 38
Foundry Lane, 62
Fox, George, 12, 13, 15, 17, 24, 32, 47, 83, 108
French, Moses, 23
Friars Walk, 27, 92
Friends Foreign Mission Association, 101
Friends Home Missionary Society, 101
Fry, Sir Edward, 82
Fuce, Joseph, 15
Fuller, Caleb, 38
Fuller, John, 32

G

Galloway, Ambrose, 14, 19, 20, 21, 27, 28, 29, 30, 32, 35, 36, 41, 43, 45
Galloway, Elizabeth, 41
Galloway, Mary, 28, 30
Galway, 81
Gardner Street, 54
Gates, Henry, 31, 35, 36, 38, 41
General Baptists, 57
Gereing, William, 21, 23
Glaisyer, Edward, 103
Glaisyer and Kemp, 69
Glaisyer, John, 67, 68, 69, 71, 94
Glaisyer, Sarah, 55, 56
Godlee, Burwood, 73, 75, 76, 78, 80, 84, 89, 96, 97, 99
Godlee, John, 65, 70, 73, 81, 104
Godlee, Mary Ann, 84, 88
Godlee, Mary Jane, 104

Godlee, Mary Rickman, 70
Godlee, Priscilla, 73, 76, 80, 85, 86
Godlee, Rickman, 73, 81
Godlee, Sarah, 70, 71, 73
Godlee, Sir Rickman, 73, 81
Grantham, Mary, 55, 56
Green, Joseph, 71
Grey Friars, 11
Grindletonians, 12
Grinstead, 31, 44
Grover, John, 14
Guernsey, 66

H

Hack, Daniel, 86
Hack, Daniel Prior, 89
Halcomb, John, 31
Hamsey, 78
Harben, Thomas, 66
Hardiman, John, 62
Harrison, Benjamin, 71
Harrison, Thomas, 31
Harrison, William, 23
Hastings line, 75
Haughton, Elizabeth, 81
Head of Brighton School of Art, 92
Heaver, John, 37, 39
Henry VIII, 11
Henshaw, Benjamin, 44
Herstmonceux, 54, 55, 56, 70
Hezekiah, 84
Hillman, 90
Hilton, Elizabeth, 20
Hilton, Tabitha, 55
Hitchin, 3, 10, 11, 74
Hodgkin, John, 70, 72, 80, 81, 94
Hodgkin, Jonathan, 80, 94
Hodgkin, Thomas, 70-72
Holbem, William, 20, 27
Hopkins, Joseph, 96, 99
Horne, John, 54, 72
Horsham, 13, 15, 25, 44, 45, 55
Horsham Gaol, 25, 44, 45
House of Correction, 44
Howard, Elizabeth, 81

I

Ifield, 14, 55
Independents, 11, 18
Irish famine, 81

J

James II, King, 5, 21, 23, 28, 29, 31, 33, 44, 45, 46, 66
Jesuits, 42
Jesus, 12, 13, 14, 17, 58, 67, 93
Joans, Walter, 31
Jubilee, Queen Victoria's, 100

K

Kemp, Caleb Rickman, 78, 94, 98
Kemp, Grover, 71, 94, 95
Kemp, Jane, 95
Kemp, William, 29
Kennard, 45
Kidd, 90
Kidder, Jane, 37, 38, 39, 40, 41
Killingbeck, Elizabeth, 14
Killingbeck, Humphrey, 14
King of Prussia, 69
Kings Bench, 44
Kingston, 25
Knight, Richard, 36, 40

L

Labrador Straits, 66
Lawcock, Thomas, 13, 14
Lawson, Thomas, 13, 14
Leighside, 75, 76, 77, 78
Letters of Marque, 66
Levellers, 12
Lewes, 14, 18, 19, 21, 23, 28, 29, 68
Lewes Baths Association, 77
Lewes Castle, 72
Lewes Dispensary, 96
Lewes Evangelical Free Church Council, 100
Lewes Savings Bank, 77
Lewes Scientific Society, 77
Lewes Subscription Library, 100
Lewes Subscription School, 59

Lewes Total Abstinence Society, 96
Lewes Town Infirmary and Dispensary, 77
Lewes Town Mission, 100
Lewesford House Academy, 74
Lidbetter, Bridger, 69
Lidbetter, Sarah, 68
Likeman, Elizabeth, 55
Likeman, Matthew Bourne, 67
London, 5, 44, 50, 53, 66, 70, 76, 81, 82, 84, 89, 99, 100, 101
London Architectural Society, 82
London City Mission, 101
Lord Northampton, 101
Lower Ouse Navigation Company, 77
Lower, Mark Anthony, 5, 50, 77
Lucas, E.V. (Edward Verrall), 86
Lucas, Edward, 86
Lucas, John Clay, 79, 94
Luckins, Richard, 44

M

Mackellow, John, 58
Macrae, 90, 94
Maidenhead, 52
Malling, 11, 29, 86
Manifestarians, 12
Mannington, Susan, 82
Mantell, Gideon, 73
Marat, Jean-Paul, 52
Maresfield, 32
Marten, Thomas, 57, 61, 62
Marten, William, 57, 58, 59, 65, 67, 68, 69
Martin, Elizabeth, 55
Martin, John, 23
Martin, Thomas, 61
Mathew, James, 21
Mechanics Institute, 77, 97
Meeting for Sufferings, 24, 43, 75, 81, 99
Middleton, Edmund, 31
Mill, John Stuart, 72
Mills, Thomas, 21
Missionary Helpers Union, 93
Mitcham, 94

Mitchell, Jane, 55
Mitchell, Jane, 55
Monday Evening Club, 97
Monk, Major, 45
Morgan, Margaret, 49
Morland, Jane, 95
Morland, John, 99
Moseley, Thomas, 27, 28, 32, 33, 35, 36, 41, 43
Movement for the Ban of the Sale of Intoxicating Liquor on Sunday, 96
Muggletonians, 12

N

National Convention, 52
Natural History Museum, 82
New Jersey, 64
Newhaven, 19, 32, 70, 76
Newington, George, 94
Newnham, Elizabeth, 55
Newnham, John, 27
Norman, Walter, 32
Norton, William, 23
Nuthurst, 14

O

Olive, John, 39
Osborn, Mary, 55, 67

P

Packer, Philip, 23, 24
Page, Richard, 31
Paine, Eliza, 79
Paine, Thomas, 50, 51, 52
Parker, Alexander, 14
Particular Baptists, 62
Payne, Eliza, 96
Pea, Captain Charles, 66
Pelham, Henry, 45
Pelham, John, 24
Pemberton, Justice, 44
Penn, William, 20
Pentonville, 70, 71
Perfect, Arthur, 88
Peters, Elizabeth, 49

Pettet, Thomas, 21
Petworth, 69
Philippe, King Louis, 76
Picknoll, Mascall, 29
Pinwell, 76, 78
Pope, the, 11, 23
Portsmouth, 69
Postlethwaite, John, 32
Postlethwaite, Walter, 18
Praemunire, 23
Presbyterians, 11
Prince of Orange, 45
Priory, 11, 83
Pry, Paul, 50
Puddle Wharf, 27, 35, 38, 39
Puritan, 11
Purser, Anne, 29
Purser, William, 28, 29

R

Randall, Francis, 20
Ranters, 12, 48
Ratcliffe Highway, 65
Read, William, 45, 46
Richardson, Ralph, 21
Rickman and Company, 94
Rickman, Aley, 54
Rickman, Ann, 54, 55
Rickman, Elizabeth, 55, 56, 70
Rickman, John, 49, 50, 53, 61, 62, 65, 71, 72, 73, 79, 80, 84, 86
Rickman, Joseph, 53
Rickman, Lucy, 53
Rickman, Mary, 55, 56, 62, 66, 70, 73
Rickman, Mary Hannah, 73, 86
Rickman, Matilda, 80
Rickman, Miss (bookseller), 51
Rickman, Nathaniel, 70
Rickman, Rachel, 80, 85, 86
Rickman, Rebecca, 54
Rickman, Richard Peters, 50, 62, 72, 73, 80, 84, 86, 96
Rickman, Samuel, 54, 62
Rickman, Sarah, 54, 84, 88
Rickman, Thomas, 61, 62, 70, 73
Ridge, 52

Rigg, Ambrose, 14
Ringmer, 72, 85
Rivers, Nisell, 21, 28
Robinson, Elizabeth, 35, 36, 41
Robinson, Elner, 20
Robinson, Maude, 5, 80, 90, 93, 95
Robinson, Thomas, 14, 29, 32, 35, 37, 38, 39, 40, 41, 43
Rochester, 89
Rotten Row, 84, 95
Rottingdean, 25, 27, 28, 43
Rowe, Walter, 45
Rowland, Thomas, 47

S

Scattergood, Thomas, 64, 65
Schnell, Emilie, 89
School Hill, 21, 45
Scrase, Henry, 21
Scrase, John, 21
Scrase, Richard, 20, 23
Scrase, Walter, 20, 23
Scripps, Edward, 30, 31
Second Conventicle Act, 27
Shaw, Margaret, 54
Shelley, Henry, 28, 35, 37, 38, 81
Shelleys, 81
Shutter, Elizabeth, 28
Shutter, John, 23
Slee, John, 13, 14
Smith, Charlotte, 80, 84
Smith, Charlotte Elizabeth, 84
Smith, Charlotte Josephine, 84
Smith, Nathan, 79
Smith, Rachel, 79
Smith, Robert, 28
Snashall, John, 50
Snatt, William, 22, 23, 28, 29
Social-Science Congress, 82
Songhurst, John, 31
Southover, 14, 15, 25, 95
Southover Church, 95
Southwark, 74
Southwick, 68
Speciall, Caroline, 79
Speciall, Mary Ann, 80, 89
Speciall, Rachel, 88, 89, 91, 93

Spencer, Christopher, 62, 68
Spicilegia, 62
St Annes, 81
St Michaels, 18
St Paul's Cathedral, 100
St Thomas, 23, 35, 39, 53, 71
Stanford, C T, 9
Stapley, Sir John, 21, 40, 43
Star Inn, 45
Stephens, Richard, 43, 44, 45
Steyning, 14
Stonehors, Richard, 39
Street, South, 36, 93
Studly, Nathaniel, 19
Sturt, Charles, 79, 80, 83
Sussex Archaeological Society, 5, 97

T

Tabernacle, 99
Tatum, John, 74
Taylor, Catherine, 80, 83, 86
The Crescent, 79, 90
The Friars, 73, 78, 86, 88
The Grey House, 86
Thomas 'Clio' Rickman, 50
Thorp, Joseph, 81
Thurgood, 31
Toleration, Act of, 45
Tottenham Meeting, 81
Trusted, Catherine, 88, 89, 93
Trusted, Mary, 80, 91, 93
Tuck, John, 31
Tuppen, William, 61, 68
Twiner, William, 67
Twinham, 14

U

Unitarians, 12

V

Vandike, John, 32
Verall, Thomas, 44
Verrall, George, 62

Verrall, Mary, 50

W

Walden, 71
Wallis, Marriage, 86, 98
Walter, John, 46
Wapping, 65
Warbleton, 14, 28, 41
Watergate Lane, 90
Waterhouse, Alfred, 82
Wealden cannon, 32
Wellingham House, 72, 84
Wenham, John, 20, 23, 25
West Indies, 94
West, Richard, 32
West, William, 32
Westgate Street, 21
Westminster, 70
White Horse Inn, 43
White Lion, 21, 22
Whyles, George, 62
Wilkason, Bryan, 14
Willard, Walter, 44
William and Mary, 23
William Yokehurst, 21
Williams, Jane née Coates, 67
Willingdon, 27, 29
Winton, Sarah, 54
Wood, Thomas, 32, 36, 39
Woods, Joseph, 82, 83
Woods, Joseph, 82, 83
Woods, Margaret, 81, 82
Workhouse, 93
Wycherley, Henry, 79

Y

Yearly Meeting, 24, 75, 81, 83, 84, 95, 99, 101, 104
YMCA, 95
Yokehurst, Nicholas, 21

Z

Zion, 65